AIR CAMPAIGN

OKINAWA 1945
The Royal Navy's biggest carrier campaign

ANGUS KONSTAM | ILLUSTRATED BY GARETH HECTOR

OSPREY PUBLISHING
Bloomsbury Publishing Plc
Kemp House, Chawley Park, Cumnor Hill, Oxford OX2 9PH, UK
Bloomsbury Publishing Ireland Limited,
29 Earlsfort Terrace, Dublin 2, D02 AY28, Ireland
1359 Broadway, 12th Floor, New York, NY 10018, USA
E-mail: info@ospreypublishing.com
www.ospreypublishing.com

OSPREY is a trademark of Osprey Publishing Ltd

First published in Great Britain in 2026

© Osprey Publishing Ltd, 2026

All rights reserved. No part of this publication may be: i) reproduced or transmitted in any form, electronic or mechanical, including photocopying, recording or by means of any information storage or retrieval system without prior permission in writing from the publishers; or ii) used or reproduced in any way for the training, development or operation of artificial intelligence (AI) technologies, including generative AI technologies. The rights holders expressly reserve this publication from the text and data mining exception as per Article 4(3) of the Digital Single Market Directive (EU) 2019/790.

A catalogue record for this book is available from the British Library.

ISBN: PB 9781472866745; eBook: 9781472866752; ePDF: 9781472866721;
XML: 9781472866738

26 27 28 29 30   10 9 8 7 6 5 4 3 2 1

Maps and Diagrams by www.bounford.com
3D BEVs by Paul Kime
Index by Angela Hall
Typeset by Lumina Datamatics Ltd
Printed by Repro India Ltd.

Title page: See caption on p. 46.

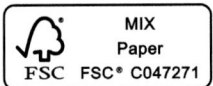

Osprey Publishing supports the Woodland Trust, the UK's leading woodland conservation charity.

To find out more about our authors and books visit www.ospreypublishing.com. Here you will find extracts, author interviews, details of forthcoming events and the option to sign up for our newsletter.
For product safety related questions contact productsafety@bloomsbury.com

AIR CAMPAIGN

CONTENTS

INTRODUCTION	4
CHRONOLOGY	6
ATTACKER'S CAPABILITIES	8
DEFENDER'S CAPABILITIES	15
CAMPAIGN OBJECTIVES	21
THE CAMPAIGN	33
AFTERMATH AND ANALYSIS	89
FURTHER READING	93
INDEX	95

INTRODUCTION

The fleet carrier HMS *Illustrious* entering the Captain Cook Graving Dock in Sydney, Australia, May 1945. In April the carrier was detached from TF 57 and was sent to Sydney for repairs. However, these proved more extensive than envisaged, and so 'Lusty' was sent on to Britain for repair and refit. The carrier was still in Rosyth when the war ended.

Until early 1944, Britain's Eastern Fleet had been starved of ships, as the Royal Navy was fully occupied fighting in other theatres closer to home – the Atlantic, the Arctic and the Mediterranean. Then, reinforcements began to arrive in the fleet's base in Ceylon, and the fleet slowly became strong enough to go over onto the offensive. At its core was a small carrier strike force which had been re-equipped with American-built aircraft. Once in the Indian Ocean, their crews were trained in American fast carrier operations – so very different from the smaller-scale carrier tactics used in European waters. From the spring of 1944 on, the Eastern Fleet launched a series of air strikes against enemy-held Sumatra, Japan's main source of the oil it needed to continue its military and naval operations. Slowly, Britain's carrier force gained experience while degrading Japan's ability to wage war.

In November, as a harbinger of things to come, the Eastern Fleet was rebranded the British Pacific Fleet (BPF). In January 1945 the successful Sumatra raids culminated in Operation *Meridian*, two large-scale air strikes against the heavily defended refineries around Palembang, the centre of oil production in Sumatra. At a stroke, Japan's oil production on the island was crippled, which consequently had a serious impact on the Japanese war effort. This though, was still a secondary objective. The real war against the Japanese was being fought elsewhere, in the Central Pacific. In February, the BPF moved its base from Trincomalee in Ceylon to Sydney in Australia, placing it closer to the centre of the action. Initially, requests to include the BPF in the US Navy's drive on Japan were rebuffed.

Then, in mid-March, the British had their way, and the BPF was invited to join the US Fifth Fleet in Operation *Iceberg* – the invasion of Okinawa, and the conquest of the Ryukyu chain of islands (or Nasei Shoto), which stretched from Formosa (now Taiwan) to the Japanese home island of Kyushu. Until then, the Pacific War fought against the forces of Imperial Japan had been almost exclusively an American conflict. The exceptions were relatively small ANZAC contingents, Australian and New Zealand forces operating on the southern fringe of this immense theatre of war. So, with the arrival of the British Pacific Fleet and its four combat-ready aircraft carriers, the Royal Navy would be fighting alongside the

In January 1945, the BPF's Carrier Strike Force ended its Sumatran bombing campaign with a two-day attack on Palembang, the centre of the island's oil production. This shows the aftermath of the first raid, which left the Pladjoe refinery ablaze. For the fleet, this was its last operation in the Indian Ocean before its transfer to the Central Pacific theatre.

US Navy, at the very epicentre of the fight. So, the BPF would play its part in this last great island invasion of the war.

What followed would be a three-month long battle against Japan's air-launched suicide attacks – its kamikaze ('Divine Wind') offensive, which turned Japan's dwindling stock of combat aircraft into piloted bombs. These posed a deadly threat to Adm. Raymond Spruance's US Fifth Fleet, which was supporting the Okinawa invasion. The kamikazes were expected to strike the US fleet from two directions – from the north, flying down from Kyushu and the northern Ryukyu chain, or from the west, from China and Formosa and on to the Sakishima Gota ('Sakishima Islands'), the western Ryukyu chain that linked Formosa and Okinawa.

The BPF, now rebranded 'Task Force 57' for the Okinawa operation, had the task of protecting the left flank of the US fleet, by neutralizing the Japanese airfields in the Sakishimas, and so denying the kamikazes a base from which they could attack Spruance's warships. To some extent this was a monotonous business, a regular pounding of these airfields to deny their use to the enemy. However, it also placed Task Force 57 in harm's way. Inevitably, the Royal Navy's carriers drew the attention of the kamikazes, and they were subjected to a series of ferocious attacks. All that stood in the way of a major naval disaster was the skill of the Task Force's air crews and sailors, and the unique armoured flight decks of the British carriers. This then, is the story of this dramatic air campaign, the longest continuous air battle ever fought by the Royal Navy.

CHRONOLOGY

1944

23–26 October Battle of Leyte Gulf – major naval victory by the US Navy, crushing the offensive capabilities of the Imperial Japanese Navy.

22 November The British Pacific Fleet (BPF) is created from elements of the British Eastern Fleet.

4 December Adm. Fraser, CINC BPF meets with Adm. Nimitz, US CINC PAC to discuss the future role of the British fleet in the Pacific theatre.

31 December The US Fifth Fleet receives orders for Operation *Iceberg* – the invasion of Okinawa.

1945

24–29 January Operation *Meridian* – Fleet Air Arm (FAA) attacks on the Palembang oil refineries.

4 February The BPF begins the relocation from its Main Base in Trincomalee in Ceylon (now Sri Lanka) to its new Main Base in Sydney, Australia.

15 February The US Navy ceded its naval facilities at Manus in the Admiralty Islands to the BPF, for use as a forward fleet base.

19 February – 19 March US invasion of Iwo Jima.

24 February Operation *Stacy* – FAA units support a naval sweep of the Adaman Sea.

28 February The BPF sails from Sydney, bound for Manus.

7 March The BPF arrives in Manus.

15 March The BPF is invited to become part of the US Fifth Fleet, prior to Operation *Iceberg*.

18 March The BPF sails from Manus, bound for the US Fifth Fleet Base at Ulithi.

18–19 March Task Force 58, US Fifth Fleet undertakes strikes on the Japanese homeland.

20–23 March The BPF is refuelled and resupplied in Ulithi.

23 March The BPF, now Task Force 57 (TF 57), sails from Ulithi, bound for the Sakishimas.

25–26 March Initial FAA air strikes on Sakishima Islands.

The Grumman Avenger proved to be a versatile strike aircraft for the Fleet Air Arm, and one which was greatly superior to earlier British-built strike aircraft. Although designed as a torpedo bomber, during the Okinawa campaign the British used their Avengers as bombers, or for anti-submarine patrols. This Avenger is shown taking off from HMS *Indefatigable* on 12 April 1945.

26 March First large kamikaze attack is launched against US Fifth Fleet.

31 March – 2 April Second round of FAA air strikes on Sakishimas.

1 April (L-1) Initial US landings on Okinawa – bridgehead established.

1–3 April Sustained series of kamikaze attacks against US Fifth Fleet.

6–7 April Third round of FAA air strikes on Sakishimas.

Heavy Japanese kamikaze attacks on US Fifth Fleet off Okinawa.

7 April Battle of East China Sea. US Task Force 58 destroys Japanese naval force off the eastern coast of Kyushu, before it attempts to attack the US fleet off Okinawa. The battleship *Yamato* is sunk.

9 April (L+8) Heavy fighting on Okinawa as US troops approach main lines of Japanese resistance.

12–13 April Operation *Iceberg Oolong* – TF 57 attacks on airfields in northern Formosa.

16–17 April Fourth round of FAA strikes on Sakishimas.

19 April (L+18) Major US offensive begins on southern portion of the island.

20 April (L+19) Fifth round of FAA air strikes on Sakishimas, prior to departure of TF 57 for Leyte. Northern portion of Okinawa is cleared of Japanese resistance.

22–30 April Sustained series of kamikaze strikes on US Third Fleet off Okinawa.

23 April – 1 May TF 57 replenishes and takes on stores in Leyte, in the Philippines.

4–5 May Sixth round of FAA air strikes in Sakishimas, combined with a naval bombardment of Miyako Island on 4 May.

4 May First Japanese kamikaze strike on Task Force – carriers *Formidable* and *Indomitable* are damaged by kamikaze hits but remain operational. The US Fifth Fleet is also attacked off Okinawa, losing two destroyers.

8–9 May Seventh round of FAA air strikes on Sakishimas.

9 May Second kamikaze strike on Task Force – carriers *Formidable* and *Victorious* damaged.

11 May US escort carrier *Bunker Hill* badly damaged in kamikaze strike off Okinawa.

12–13 May Eighth round of FAA air strikes on Sakishimas.

16 May Ninth round of FAA air strikes on Sakishimas, but worsening weather leads to cancellation of strikes for 17 May.

21–21 May Tenth round of FAA air strikes on Sakishimas.

24–25 May Final round of FAA air strikes on Sakishimas.

25 May The BPF ceases operations and returns to Manus. V. Adm. Rawlings, in fleet flagship, *King George V*, sails for Guam, to discuss future operations with Adm. Nimitz.

26 May Adm. Spruance, CINC US Fifth Fleet, praises TF 57 for its fine work and for upholding the traditions of the Royal Navy.

18–21 June (L+78–81) Collapse of organized Japanese resistance on Okinawa.

30 June (L+90) Final pockets of Japanese resistance are overcome, ending lengthy mopping-up operation.

ATTACKER'S CAPABILITIES

The Vought Corsair was modified slightly for the Fleet Air Arm, with a bulged canopy fitted, to raise the pilot's seat and so improve visibility, which was limited, especially during take-off and landing. The Royal Navy though, liked this rugged, robust and dependable fighter, which had a greater range than the British-built Seafire.

In December 1944, as his fleet was still conducting an intensive air campaign against Japanese-held Sumatra, the future of the British fleet hung in the balance. Adm. Fraser, Commander-in-Chief of the British Pacific Fleet (CINC BPF), met Adm. Chester Nimitz and Adm. Spruance, to discuss how the British and American fleets might work together. By this stage of the war, the American Pacific Fleet was a highly professional entity, having gained its experience in the crucible of war. The British too, were battle-hardened and professional, but their combat experience had been gained in other theatres, against very different enemies. Above all, the core of the American offensive power in the Pacific was its fast carrier fleet, which had won a string of victories, and in the process had broken the back of its Japanese opponents. Along the way, the US Navy had become experts in fast carrier operations – a skill the British were only just beginning to embrace. Both Nimitz and Spruance though, were keen to have the BPF fight alongside them, especially if they could accommodate the different procedures and practices of their British allies.

One of the weakest features of the British Pacific Fleet in early 1945 was its Fleet Train. This was the assembly of vessels which provided logistical support for the BPF, from refuelling at sea and the supply of fuel, ammunition and stores, to the floating maintenance and repair facilities it needed. In the US Pacific Fleet, with seemingly unlimited resources the task forces were served by a large, modern logistical support fleet, whose efficiency had been honed and perfected over years of campaigning in the Pacific. These support vessels, from fleet oilers used to replenish the warships to the storeships and maintenance vessels were almost all modern and purpose-built, or at least had been heavily converted for the task.

By contrast the British Fleet Train was made up of a range of vessels, some of which were designed for the purpose, but many were merchant ships which had been pressed into service and hastily modified to fit the Admiralty's requirements. Given Britain's shortage of merchant ships and merchant seamen after six years of war, it was hardly surprising that many of these were far from perfectly suited for the purpose. The Main Base of the BPF was Sydney in Australia, 4,000 miles to the south of the Sakishima Islands. The fuel, supplies and other material needs of the fleet were transported from there to the BPF's Advance Base at Manus in the Admiralty Islands, halfway between Sydney and the fleet's Operational Area.

The Operational Area itself wasn't technically the location of the fleet itself while in action – its Operating Area or 'Flying-off Point – but an area well to the south, beyond the reach of enemy air attack. In this case it was an area in the Philippine Sea, defined by a map reference and a code word. This was where the fleet was refuelled, took on stores and replacement aircraft, and transferred the wounded for passage back to a hospital. Between the Main Base, the Advance Base and the Operating Area, the commander of the Fleet Train would maintain a constant shuttle of supply ships to ensure that the fleet had what it needed when it rendezvoused with the Fleet Train in one of these Operating Areas. The replenishment procedure involved the BPF withdrawing overnight from its flying-off point to the pre-arranged Operational Area, where it would meet the waiting ships of the Fleet Train.

In the US Navy, after years of practice, replenishment at sea (RAS) was a speedy process, where fleet oilers could usually replenish up to two warships at once, one on each beam of the tanker. The transfer of fuel by fuel lines was speeded up by an efficient pumping system, custom built for the purpose. As a result, a US Task Group, the equivalent size of the British Pacific Fleet, could refuel in about half a day. At the same time, the warships waiting to refuel would take on stores and accomplish all of the other requirements of the replenishment process. By contrast the British were relative newcomers to RAS, as they had almost always operated within range of a friendly naval base. While refuelling was adopted during the war, the procedure was rarely practised before the BPF entered the Pacific theatre. So, the Royal Navy crews were less skilled in RAS procedures than their American counterparts.

Adm. Fraser (in whites), CINC of the BPF, shakes the hand of Adm. Nimitz, US CINC PAC. Standing behind Fraser during this formal greeting ceremony in early 1945, is Adm. Spruance, commander of the US Fifth Fleet, under whom the British fleet will serve.

In 1945, the Royal Navy crews of TF 57 were relative newcomers to replenishment at sea (RAS), as this was rarely needed in western waters. The British also suffered from a lack of custom-built tankers, and usually had to make do with ones hastily adapted from merchant vessels. As a result, RAS took much longer for TF 57 than it did for its US colleagues. Here, a destroyer pulls away from *Illustrious* after refuelling from the carrier.

OPPOSITE THE AIR DEFENCE OF TF 57

The initial warning of an approaching air attack came from the fleet's Airborne Early Warning Radars (the British Type 281, Type 279 and American SM-1 sets), which had various ranges and capabilities, but could track enemy aircraft (or 'bogeys') effectively 60 miles from the TF. This would be monitored by the Fighter Direction Officer and their teams in the carriers, and they would direct the placement of the Combat Air Patrol (CAP). The CAP usually consisted of 16 Seafires from 887 and 894 Naval Air Squadrons (NAS), operating from *Indefatigable*. Two pairs would be sent to patrol positions on the opposite side of the TF from the approaching 'bogeys', in case other enemy aircraft approached without being detected.

A Fairey Firefly fighter-bomber landing on the deck of a carrier, being grabbed by the aircraft handling party, after being brought to a halt by the aircraft's tailhook and one of the carrier's six arrester wires. In the British Pacific Fleet (BPF), the two-man Firefly was exclusively flown by 1770 Naval Air Squadron (NAS), embarked in HMS *Indefatigable*. The BPF adopted the American marking system, where the '2' indicated an aircraft with a two-man crew. The 'S' on the tail indicated the aircraft's parent carrier was *Indefatigable*.

The British also lacked the specialist fleet tankers available to their allies. Even Royal Fleet Auxiliary (RFA) tankers were less efficient than American ones, lacking the fittings, pumps and equipment that permitted high-speed refuelling at sea. The Merchant Navy tankers used by the Royal Navy in the Pacific were even more poorly equipped, and their crews were less adept at RAS techniques than their RFA or RN counterparts. Due to all this, the British tended to refuel using the refuelling astern method, where fuel lines were passed to warships following astern, rather than on its beam. This then limited the recipient to one vessel at a time. Consequently, the lack of experience, the poor and often makeshift equipment and the non-specialist crews led to lengthy delays. As a result, it usually took the BPF two days to undertake a full fuelling of the fleet. Consequently, this more than doubled the time spent by the fleet away from its active operational duties.

Until 1944, the Royal Navy's Fleet Air Arm had been poorly served in terms of aircraft. However, by the close of the Sumatra campaign, most of its British-designed aircraft had been replaced by American ones, which were, in the main, a marked improvement on their predecessors. The Vought Corsair and Grumman Hellcat were both superb fighters, which greatly boosted the combat potential of the British carrier fleet. The main strike arm was also centred around an American-designed aircraft, the Grumman Avenger. Although this was a torpedo bomber, it also served as an excellent dive bomber. As the British fleet operating off Okinawa would be fighting an air campaign against land-based targets, the Avenger squadrons – one in each British carrier – would be used exclusively as bombers. Their weakness, if any, lay in their ordnance, which was ideal for bombing the *Tirpitz* in a Norwegian fjord, but less suitable for bombing softer-surfaced Japanese airfields.

British aircraft carriers also used a number of British aircraft, a new generation of designs based on wartime experience. The Supermarine Seafire was effectively the naval version of the celebrated Spitfire. While still an extremely potent fighter, it was somewhat too fragile for the rough handling involved in carrier operations. It also lacked the endurance of the

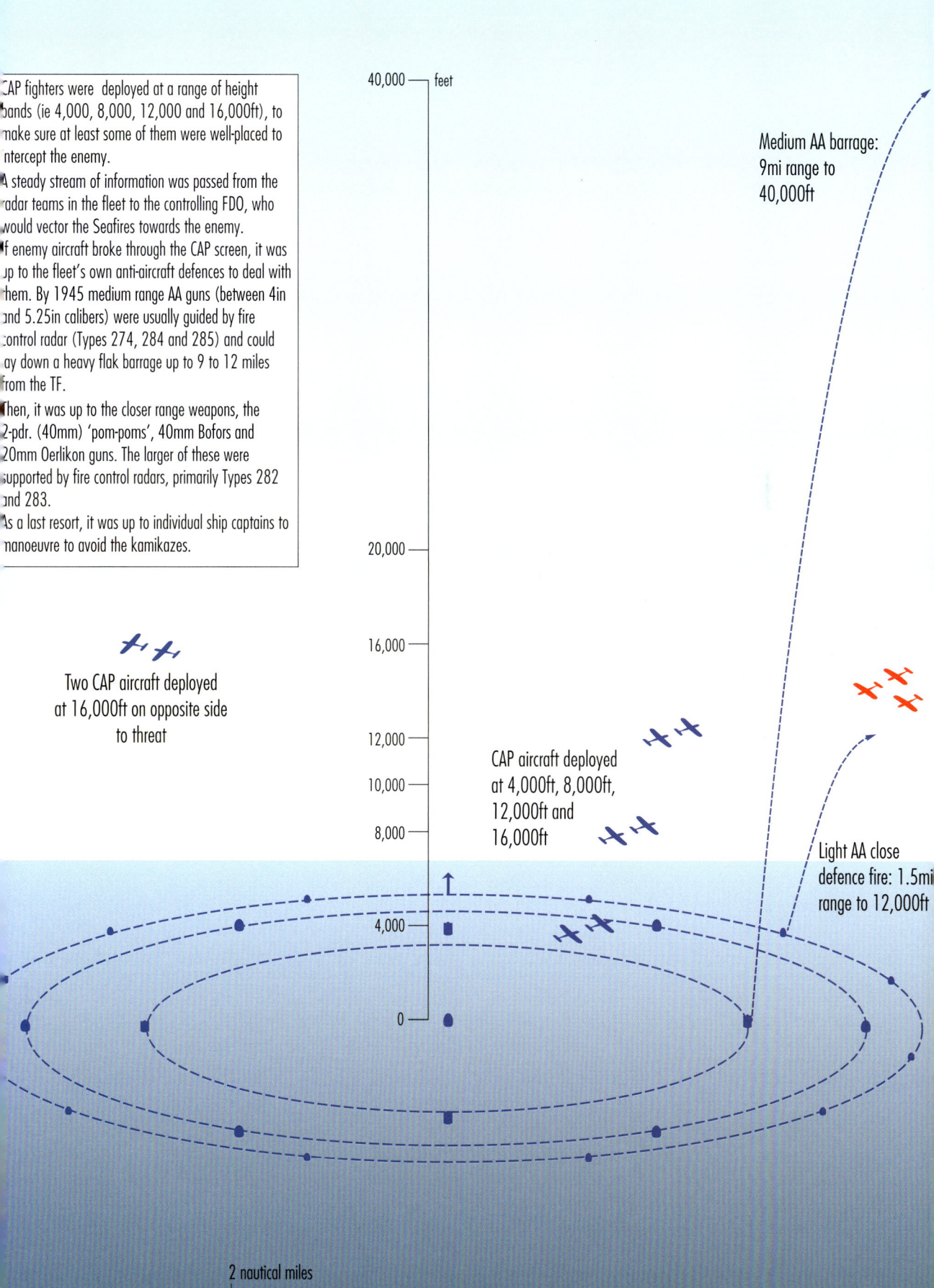

latest American fighters. As a result, Seafires were only embarked in one British carrier, *Indefatigable*, and these were primarily used to provide Combat Air Patrol (CAP) cover for the fleet. A far larger and more robust aircraft was the Fairey Firefly, a fighter-bomber which was ideal for carrier operations, with a versatility that gave it a range of roles, from strike aircraft to fighter.

The British carriers themselves were markedly different from their American counterparts. While the latter had wooden flight decks, the British ones had thick steel ones, rendering them far more resilient to damage. HMS *Illustrious*, namesake of her class, together with her sisters HMS *Formidable* and HMS *Victorious*, displaced just over 28,000 tons, and had all seen extensive service in the Mediterranean. In early 1941, *Illustrious* had taken seven bomb hits and still remained afloat, thanks to her armour, which not only protected the flight deck, but also the sides of her hangars. After being repaired in the United States, she returned to service, but this time she was taking on a new opponent in the Far East. A variant of the Illustrious class of fleet carriers was HMS *Indomitable*, whose designers had exchanged some of her armour for additional hangar space. The Implacable class represented a further development, a slightly larger 32,000-ton version of *Illustrious*, which could accommodate more aircraft, but at the cost of a lower hangar height, which prevented the use of the larger American fighters. In the Pacific, the class was represented by HMS *Indefatigable*. Due to that hangar height problem, *Indefatigable* embarked Seafires.

These armoured flight decks proved a real boon in the Okinawa campaign. Their advantage was best summed up by a US Navy liaison officer, who was on board *Indomitable* during the aftermath of a kamikaze attack in May 1945. He declared, 'When a Kamikaze hits a US carrier, it's six months repair at Pearl. In a Limey carrier, it's a case of "Sweepers, man your brooms"!' While this was a slight exaggeration, it demonstrated the point that the armoured flight decks proved their worth when these carriers were attacked by kamikazes. This resilience though, came at a price. The armour took up space which might otherwise have been used to house aircraft. So, while a US Navy carrier might embark 90 aircraft, their British counterparts embarked air wings of between 44 and 55 aircraft. The exception was *Indefatigable*, which could embark 69 aircraft. The result was that Task Force 57 possessed much fewer aircraft than a typical US Navy Task Group.

The Illustrious-class fleet carrier HMS *Victorious*, pictured prior to her deployment to the Central Pacific. During Operation *Iceberg*, and for the rest of the war, the carrier sported a much simpler scheme, of light grey overall, with the port lower hull painted dark blue and the starboard side a mid-blue panel, which covered the central two-thirds of the lower hull.

In contrast to the British fleet carriers, the carriers of the US Carrier Strike Force had wooden rather than armoured steel flight decks, which rendered them more vulnerable to damage from kamikaze strikes. The carrier shown here is the USS *Essex*, which formed part of US TF 58.

By this stage of the war the British were extremely well equipped with radar. A combination of the latest British and American air warning sets were able to detect approaching Japanese 'bogeys' (radar contacts) at ranges of more than 120 miles, although they were unable to spot extremely low-flying aircraft approaching them. These sets could also give the defenders information on the height of the enemy aircraft, as well as speed and the number of aircraft. The Flight Control Officer for the fleet aboard *Indefatigable* was then able to direct the fighters of the CAP stationed over the carriers to intercept the enemy planes. The CAP fighters themselves, usually numbering around 16 to 20 aircraft, were ordered to patrol at set altitudes, of between 2,000ft and 20,000ft, so they were able to intercept approaching aircraft regardless of their height.

Once the enemy came within range of the task force, the formation it was sailing in would come into its own. During this campaign, the BPF adopted the US Navy style of deployment. A cruiser served as the guide in the centre of the formation, while other ships were stationed at set distances from the guide, forming a series of defensive rings. The inner ring, approximately a mile from the guide, consisted of the carriers, usually deployed at 90°, 180°, 270° and 360° from the guide cruiser. A mile and a half to two miles from the guide was the second ring, made up of the fleet's battleships and cruisers. Then, around four miles from the guide, was the third circle, made up of the fleet's destroyers. During the latter stages of the campaign a destroyer was stationed directly astern of each of the carriers, to provide additional firepower during kamikaze attacks. It was found that the kamikaze pilots favoured a stern approach, and this helped cover this vulnerable spot. The fleet's AA cruisers were also moved closer to the carriers to improve their AA coverage.

During the Okinawa campaign the modified Illustrious-class fleet carrier HMS *Indefatigable* had her camouflage scheme repainted to conform to the standard for the Pacific Fleet – light grey overall, with a dark blue lower hull. Unlike the other fleet carriers, she had Supermarine Seafires embarked, which were used to provide the Task Force's CAP.

Also during the final stages of the campaign, Task Force 57 adopted the American practice of stationing a radar picket around 12 miles from the fleet. While the Americans usually used a destroyer for this, the British used a cruiser, supported by a destroyer, with its own dedicated CAP flying overhead. These radar pickets served two purposes. The first was to provide early warning of an approaching air attack. Secondly, as it was known there were Japanese radar units in the Sakishimas, air strikes launched from the carrier tended to head towards the pickets after taking off from the carriers or returning to them. This made it harder for the Japanese to determine exactly where the flying-off point of the Task Force was sited.

Once an approaching air strike was located on radar, and if enemy aircraft were able to evade the CAP screen, then the Task Force's own AA defences would take over. In most cases, these AA weapons were linked to fire-control radar systems, allowing an accurate and coordinated barrage of fire to be sent up. As the attacking aircraft came within range, the larger guns would be augmented by close-range AA weapons, such as 20mm and 40mm weapons, designed to target specific attackers. During kamikaze attacks, there were several instances where the approaching aircraft was hit multiple times and shot down during its final dive towards a carrier. There were drawbacks though, as on occasion friendly fire incidents took place, as CAP fighters pursuing kamikazes flew into the arc of fire of these close-range defensive weapons.

Despite the limitations of its logistical support, the British Pacific Fleet was a highly efficient force, crewed for the most part by highly professional and widely experienced officers and men. The carrier force might have been a relative newcomer to US-style Fast Carrier Operations, but it had perfected these methods in the Indian Ocean during the Sumatra campaign of 1944–45. It was well led by highly competent and experienced commanders – Fraser, Rawlings and Vian had all proved their worth in actions and naval victories in the Barents Sea, the Atlantic and the Mediterranean. The fleet's Carrier Strike Force was composed of four British fleet carriers which had seen extensive action, and which, by the spring of 1945, were equipped with a powerful air wing. While the strike force lacked the size of an equivalent American one, this was balanced by the increased defensive qualities of the carriers themselves. As a result, the British Pacific Fleet – or Task Force 57 – was a highly capable force, whose officers and men were out to prove their worth in the eyes of their American counterparts. By the end of the campaign, they more than achieved this, earning the right to serve alongside the US Navy again, during the final drive on the Japanese homeland.

DEFENDER'S CAPABILITIES

By this stage of the war in the Pacific, the Japanese were defending their own territory in the Ryushu Islands, rather than places they'd occupied early in the conflict. So, they were expected to fight ferociously to repel the Allied invaders, or at the very least make them pay a high price for their capture of Okinawa.

Okinawa itself was strongly garrisoned, with two infantry divisions (24th and 62nd), an independent mixed brigade (44th Mixed Brigade) and an assortment of supporting troops including the 27th Tank Regiment. They were all at the disposal of Gen. Mitsuru Ujijima, Commander-in-Chief of the Japanese 32nd Army, whose headquarters was on Okinawa. He had responsibility for commanding the garrisons of all of the Ryushu island chain, including the Sakishima Guntō.

The 57-year-old Ujijima, a native of Kagoshima, was an intelligent officer, whose 37 military years had involved staff, command and instructing experience. In 1937 he became a major general, and commanded a brigade with great skill around Shanghai and Wuhan during the Second Sino-Japanese War campaign. By 1939, he'd been promoted and given command of a division. His opposition to the war with the United States led to him being sidelined, and posted to the Ryushus, which were regarded as something of a backwater until the spring of 1945. He heavily fortified the southern portion of the island and was as prepared as he could be for the American onslaught when it came. In all, including Army Air Force and Imperial Navy detachments, Ujijima had just over 77,000 troops under his command. Most of these though, were deployed on Okinawa itself.

The Nakajima Ki-44 fighters *Shoki* ('Devil Vanquisher') or 'Army Type 2' fighter, was codenamed 'Tojo' by the Allies. In the spring of 1945 they were deployed in Formosa by the Japanese 8th Air Division, and used as fast interceptors to take on Allied bombers. During Operation *Iceberg*, several were destroyed on the ground in both Formosa and the Sakishimas.

Sakishima military defences

As part of the 32nd Army's area, the real flaw in Japanese dispositions was the establishment of the army command in Okinawa – the strongest of the Ryukyu Islands, but also the one most likely to become a prime target for amphibious assault. Once Operation *Iceberg* began, the defenders of the Sakishima Islands were largely left to their own devices. Their military strength, although smaller than that of Okinawa, was still sufficient to give any invader pause for thought.

Miyako Jima garrison

This consisted of the 28th Infantry Division, made up of a headquarters, two infantry regiments (3rd and 30th), a cavalry regiment (28th), a mountain artillery regiment (28th), as well as divisional units of engineers, signals, medical, transport and supply units. The total strength was approximately 10,000 men. In addition, two independent mixed brigades were stationed on the island (28th and 59th Brigades), each made up of four battalions of infantry, a mortar battalion and engineer and signal units. The total strength of each brigade was around 3,000 men. In addition, the garrison included a tank company (with 12 obsolete 'I-Go' medium tanks), two machine-gun and one rapid-fire battalions (with 25mm quick-fire guns), an artillery regiment (with 12 150mm howitzers deployed as coastal batteries), engineers and two sea-raider (or commando) battalions. There was also a small airfield defence unit (205th) and an airfield construction unit (129th). In all, the garrison was around 20,000 strong.

Ishigaki Jima garrison

This island had a much smaller garrison, centred around the 45th Independent Mixed Brigade. It was made up of five rather than four infantry battalions, as well as engineers, a machine-gun battalion, a rapid-fire company and a heavy artillery regiment. These then came to around 3,500 men. In addition, the 69th Airfield Battalion protected the island's three airfields, supported by the 128th Airfield Construction Unit, with a total strength of around 500 men. Various independent construction, repair and medical units boosted numbers by another 500 men, giving a total available Japanese military manpower on Ishigaki of 4,500 men.

Compared to Okinawas though, the Sakishima Islands were only lightly garrisoned, and their defences were minimal, compared to the in-depth network of bunkers, tunnels and trenches created on Ujijima's orders on Okinawa. Despite this, the two islands were well served by specially constructed barracks, fuel dumps, field hospitals, anti-aircraft defences around the airfields, sanitation units, transport pools and security details. One interesting addition was

The whole aim of the Sakishima operation was the bombing of the airfields in the island chain. The largest of them was Hirara on Miyako Jima. Here, the main target is the spot where the airfield's three coral-paved runways intersected.

the two radar stations, one on each island, manned by the 32nd Army Air Intelligence Unit, attached to Gen. Ujijima's headquarters.

Anti-aircraft defences

The three airfields on Ishigaki Jima (Ishigaki Main, Miyara and Hegina) were defended by a sizeable detachment of two independent AA artillery battalions (74th and 82nd), while the 74th AA Battalion provided a sizeable detachment charged with defending the airfields on Miyako Jima (Hirara, Sukuma and Nobara). In all, 26 heavy (75mm or 90mm) and 66 light (20mm or occasionally 37mm) AA guns were emplaced around Ishigaki Main, while 12 heavy and 54 light AA guns were sited around the other main airfield in the islands, Hirara, on Miyako Jima. The remaining two airfields on Ishigaki and the two on Miyako each had 18–24 light AA guns emplaced around the airfields. During the course of the British Pacific Fleet air campaign, more light AA guns were shipped to the Sakishimas from Formosa, and although the exact number of these cannot be determined, it has been estimated that these amounted to around 32 extra light AA guns for Ishigaki and 26 more for Miyako.

Each of the three main islands had an air warning station, supported by a network of radio direction masts on Yonakuni, Iriomote, Ishigaki and Miyako. More significantly, both Ishigaki and Miyako had a radar station at the centre of the island, detached from the visual air warning station. On Miyako the 2nd Independent Radar Unit detachment used a Tachi Type 18 Air Warning Radar antenna, which in theory had a range of approximately 125 miles. The set on Ishigaki manned by the 32nd Army Radar was probably a Tachi 7 'Otsu' set. These radars had two drawbacks. First, the device was troublesome and sensitive, and the repeated bombing of Ishigaki and Miyako meant that the sets were often put out of action owing to severed power lines or damaged equipment. For the same reason the second flaw was the transmission of sighting reports. The original command structure had them sent to 32nd Army Headquarters on Okinawa, but after Operation *Iceberg* began, this proved impossible. So, a more circuitous route had to be found, relayed on to Formosa. However, the sets did warn the defenders of impending raids and helped build up a picture of the location of the British Task Force's flying-off point, which was then passed on to Formosa, which in turn was used to direct kamikaze attacks against the British fleet.

Aircraft

For the most part the Japanese aircraft deployed against Task Force 57 operated from airfields on Formosa. They were part of the 8th Air Division, which was based on the island, which had its headquarters in Taipei, near Matsuyama airfield. The division was made up of three Air Brigades ('Hikōdan'), each made up of two Air Combat Groups ('Hikō Sentai') of three squadrons. Each Air Combat Group used a single type of aircraft, either bombers or fighters. In addition, there were a number of independent squadrons on Formosa, mainly consisting of reconnaissance or maritime patrol aircraft or transport formations. The fighters stationed on Formosa were primarily 'Oscars' and 'Zekes', as well as the larger 'Tojo' heavy fighter.

In all, there were 14 Japanese airfields in northern Formosa and ten more in the south of the island. The principal ones for staging potential air attacks on the British Task Force were Matsuyama, Shinchiku, Koko and Tosei, the latter being the main fighter airfield at the northern end of the 230-mile-long island. The Division was part of the Japanese First Air Army, commanded by Lt Gen. Prince Yi Un, whose headquarters was in Tokyo's Seikei University building. On 1 April, in the aftermath of the Okinawa invasion, the Prince was replaced by Lt Gen. Takeo Yasuda, a keen advocate of the use of kamikaze attacks. The 10th Air Division was stationed in the Japanese Home Islands, and was based in Tokyo. While its primary function was to defend the Home Islands from attack, it was also available for offensive operations over the north-eastern Ryukyu Islands, including Okinawa.

DEFENDER'S CAPABILITIES

OPPOSITE KAMIKAZE STRIKES ON THE CARRIER STRIKE FORCE, TF 57, 1 APRIL, 4 MAY & 9 MAY, 1945

Despite all the defensive measures taken by TF 57, in this attack, some kamikaze pilots evaded the CAP fighters and reached the carriers. They either flew just above sea level to avoid being detected on radar, or approached detected but unseen using the cover of the clouds. These 'bogeys' usually appeared on radar just a minute or less from the TF. Most climbed to around 3,000ft and were identified as 'Zeke' (or Zero) fighters. Their direct course and 250kg bomb marked them out as kamikaze planes. They were then subjected to the TF's anti-aircraft defences, both flak barrages thrown up by the medium guns and then close-range fire. While some kamikazes were shot down, a few managed to reach their final target.

The total aircraft available to the Japanese Army Air Force in this campaign was as follows.

Total aircraft available to JAAF					
	Fighters	Bombers	Medium bombers	Light bombers	Float planes
Japanese homeland	1,200	300	450	30	250
Ryukyu Islands	24	12	12	-	30
Formosa	110	36	60	10	90
Mainland China	200	30	24	50	150

In addition, the Imperial Japanese Naval Air Force had approximately the following number of aircraft available in the theatre, largely based in the Japanese homeland, but with other formations in Formosa. The totals given below exclude aircraft in storage or under repair.

Aircraft available for the IJNAF						
	Fighters	Naval Dive bombers	Naval torpedo bombers	Land-based bombers	Float planes	Flying boats
Naval Air Force	2,220	362	362	413	664	67

The Ryukyu Islands had relatively few Japanese Air Force aircraft stationed at its airfields; just two squadrons of fighters, one of A6M Zero ('Zeke') and the other of Ki-43 Hayabusa ('Oscar') aircraft, all of which were at Yontan and Kadena airfields on Okinawa. A squadron of G4M1 ('Betty') bombers was also based at Kadena. At Ishigaki Main in the Sakishimas, there was a squadron of D4Y1 'Suisei' ('Judy') dive bombers serving as maritime reconnaissance aircraft. These fell under the 36th Air Brigade's command, of the 10th Air Division, but after

On 4 May, the fleet carrier HMS *Formidable* was struck by a kamikaze, just beside the forward part of the carrier's island. When the Zeke fighter and its bomb exploded, the blast cracked open the carrier's superstructure, causing carnage in the sick bay on the deck level of the island.

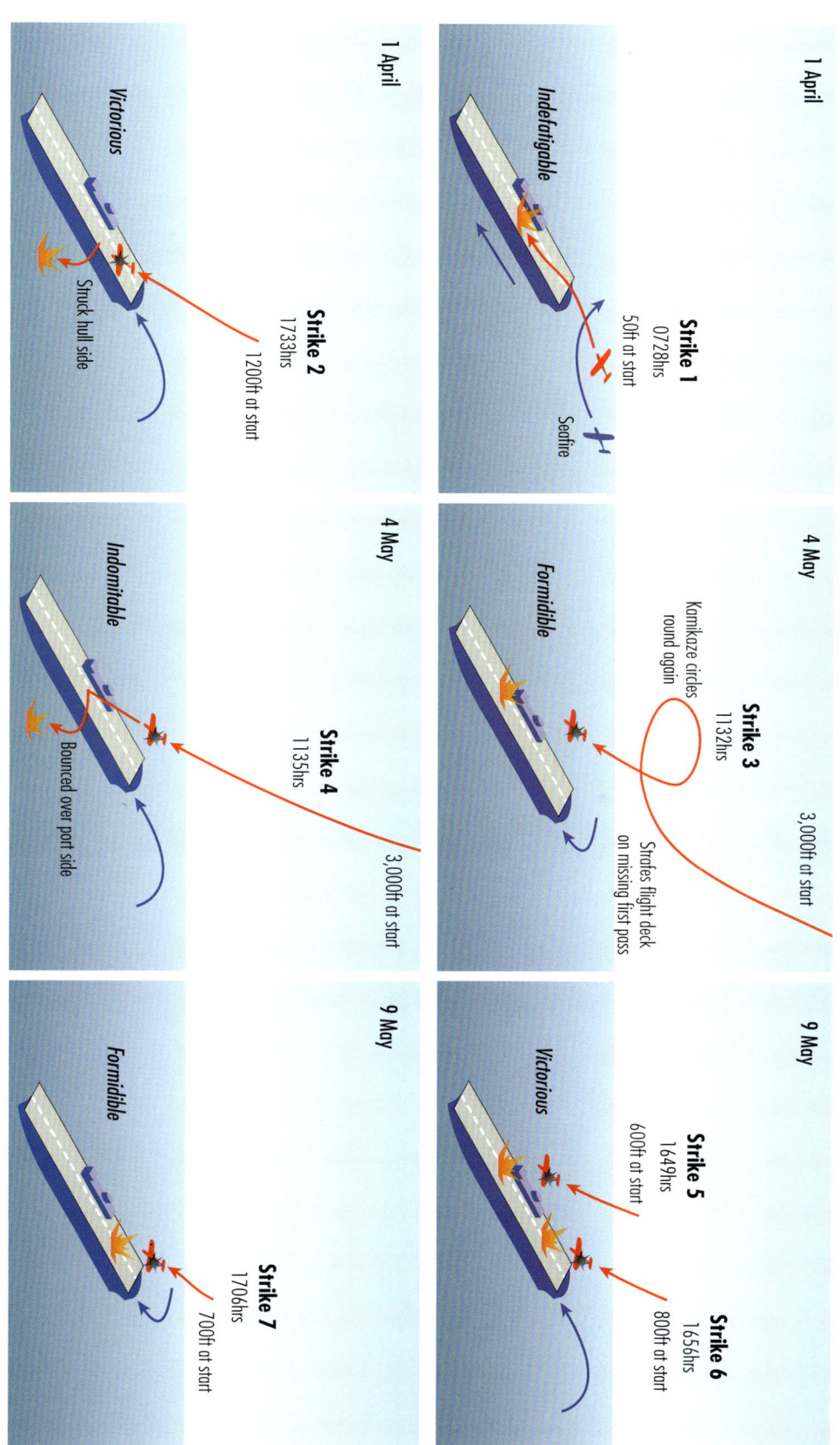

Strike 1: On 1 April *Indefatigable* was hit by a kamikaze, despite the Seafire being set ablaze by a Seafire.
Strike 2: That evening *Victorious* suffered a glancing blow by a Zeke that hit the edge of her flight deck but exploded in the sea.
Strikes 3 & 4: *Indomitable* was hit on 4 May, when a kamikaze 'bounced' off her flight deck into the sea. Minutes earlier *Formidable* had been strafed by a kamikaze which couldn't alight properly for a deck strike. The plane calmly circled around then crashed onto the flight deck.
Strikes 5 & 6: At 1649hrs on 9 May, a Zeke approaching *Victorious* at low altitude, exploded in a fireball on the forward end of her flight deck. Minutes later, at 1656hrs, *Victorious* was struck again. Despite turning away, a Zeke crashed onto the flight deck, exploding among a group of Corsairs.
Strike 7: Ten minutes later, a Zeke crashed into *Formidable* and wrecked several aircraft on the flight deck.

In all cases, all flying operations were resumed the following day by TF 57. Decks were cleared of debris, and dents filled in with concrete. It was almost as if the British armoured carrier had been designed as a foil to the kamikazes.

Okinawa was invaded, operational control of any remaining aircraft was passed to the 8th Air Division on Formosa. The real threat to TF 57 came from two sources. The first was the conventional air units of the 8th Air Division, operating from airfields on Formosa. They also carried out attacks on the US Fifth Fleet off Okinawa, some 330 to 350 miles from Matsuyama airfield near Taipei. By passing well to the north of the Sakishimas, they could reach the American warships while largely avoiding TF 57.

During Operation *Iceberg*, the Japanese 8th Air Division on Formosa was reinforced by aircraft transferred from mainland China. Japanese airfields in Zhejiang and Guangdong provinces were within easy reach of Formosa, and from there reinforcing air units could be thrown into the fight against the Allied invaders. For the most part though, this conduit for reinforcements was primarily used to move *tokko* ('special attack') units into position for attacks on both the American and British fleets operating off the Ryushus. It was these special attack formations – the kamikazes – that posed the single greatest air threat to the Allied fleets.

The kamikaze threat

The Japanese first resorted to using suicide tactics in late 1944, in response to the American invasion of Leyte in the Philippines. These tactics displayed the desperation of the Japanese High Command by this stage of the war, and its determination to turn the tide. They also showed the high sense of patriotism and duty among Japanese servicemen. The term '*tokko*' was used to encompass all such suicide or *kamikaze* ('divine wind') attacks, whether carried out on land, at sea or in the air. By the summer of 1944, the Japanese Navy began to seriously consider the use of airborne *tokko* units, as a means of overcoming its numerical weakness. By this stage of the war, experienced Japanese naval pilots were in short supply. However, a suicidal rash attack could be carried out by a less experienced pilot, if his attack was pressed home with determination. So, in October 1944 the Kamikaze Special Attack unit was formed, and proved effective in attacks on US Navy warships. The scheme was expanded, and by January 400 Army Air Force and 436 navy kamikaze pilots and aircraft had been expended. As well as air *tokko* units, suicide crash boats were also used in the Philippines, with mixed results. Both would be used more extensively against the US Fifth Fleet off Okinawa.

V. Adm. Matome Ugaki, Commander of the Japanese 5th Air Fleet, was given the task of coordinating the kamikaze counter-attack against the Americans off Okinawa. His air fleet consisted of naval air units, primarily made up of fighters, and many of these were expended in kamikaze attacks during the Fifth Fleet's attacks on the Japanese homeland, and during Operation *Iceberg*. For the most part, kamikaze units, whether operating from Kyushu in the Japanese homeland or Formosa, flew in specially converted Zero or Zeke fighters. These usually carried as large a bomb as possible, and were adapted so that the flying controls could be set so the aircraft continued its dive even if the pilot had been killed or incapacitated. The success of a kamikaze attack though, was often a matter of luck.

During the campaign, 2,000 Japanese kamikaze pilots sacrificed themselves, but in the process, they inflicted considerable damage on the enemy. A total of 26 Allied ships were sunk, most of them destroyers, transports or landing craft. Some 4,900 Allied sailors were killed and 4,824 wounded. In addition, 164 Allied ships were damaged. This total included the British carriers *Formidable*, *Indefatigable* and *Victorious*. The American carriers *Bunker Hill*, *Hancock* and *Intrepid* were also hit, along with the escort carrier *Sangamon*, as were the battleships *Maryland*, *Nevada* and *Tennessee*. However, these larger warships proved hard to sink. This was especially so of the British armoured carriers, which were notably resilient to kamikaze attacks. In the end though, this suicidal attrition tactic would fail, as, despite the high casualty list, these attacks did little to reduce the offensive potential of the US Fifth Fleet – or for that matter Task Force 57.

CAMPAIGN OBJECTIVES
The strategic picture

During America's counter-attack in the Pacific the emphasis had been on securing the South-West Pacific, to safeguard strategic links with Australia and the Indian Ocean, and the Aleutian Islands, to protect Alaska. The US Navy's victory at Midway in June 1942 guaranteed the security of its great naval base at Pearl Harbor and gave the Americans the freedom to develop their counter-punch in the Solomon Islands. From there, while the Australians and US Army were embroiled in a hard-fought campaign in New Guinea, the first 'island-hopping' operations were carried out in the Central Pacific, at Tarawa, Makin Atoll and Kwajalein in the Gilbert and Marshall Islands. The prospect of operations around Iwo Jima and Okinawa were far from the minds of US planners, whose attention was occupied elsewhere.

The capture of the Mariana Islands – Saipan, Tinian and Guam – safeguarded American supply lines and gave the US Navy access to the Philippine Sea. Then, the US Navy's decisive victory at the Battle of the Philippine Sea (13–19 June 1944) broke the offensive power of the Imperial Japanese Navy and paved the way for a return to the Philippines, which the Americans had been driven from two years earlier. While American strategists debated the value of a landing in the Philippines or Formosa, another plan emerged, based around the development of an attack on Japan itself. Iwo Jima in the Volcano archipelago lay astride an arc of islands that ran northwards through the Pacific from the Marianas to Japan. This was the path used by US Air Force bombers to attack Japan, and the neutralization of Japanese airfields on Iwo Jima would reduce bomber casualties. It would also give the Americans an airbase much closer to Tokyo.

So, while Gen. MacArthur convinced his superiors to approve an attack on the Philippines, while bypassing the Dutch East Indies, the invasion of Iwo Jima was also sanctioned. However, Okinawa in the Ryukyu Islands was much closer to the Japanese Home Islands. The Ryukyus curved down from the Japanese home island of Kyushu down to Formosa, off the Chinese coast. Okinawa in the centre of this chain was an important Japanese air base. In American hands, it would safeguard the flank of the attack on the Philippines and

Before a strike could be launched the aircraft had to be brought up in a lift from the hangar deck, then ranged into place on the after end of the flight deck, ready for flying off. There the wings would be unfolded, the aircraft checked, fuelled and armed, and then the airmen would clamber aboard. By the spring of 1945, these Fairey Barracudas embarked in Indomitable *had been replaced by Grumman Avengers.*

OPPOSITE THE THEATRE OF OPERATIONS, 1945

Before the start of Operation *Iceberg*, carriers of the BPF are seen at anchor in Seeadler Harbour, Manus, in the Admiralty Islands, which served as the forward base of the BPF. In the foreground is HMS *Formidable*, making smoke, with HMS *Indomitable* astern of her.

would serve as a superb base for American airpower during the final assault on the Japanese homeland. The scale of both amphibious attacks was enormous, but by then the US Navy was highly experienced in these kinds of operations, and had the strength, firepower and logistical support to make them succeed.

Plans for these assaults were developed in early 1945, but the attacks were postponed because of delays in MacArthur's reconquest of Luzon in the Philippines and the recapture of Manila. However, on 19 February, US Marines landed on Iwo Jima, supported by the US Navy, and US Air Force bombers operating from Saipan. The final Japanese resistance on the island was overcome on 26 March. Then, it was the turn of Okinawa. This assault would involve the specially formed 10th Army, made up of two Corps, one of US marines and the other of US Army soldiers. The bulk of the US Fifth Fleet would support these land forces with naval bombardments and carrier-based air strikes. The initial plans called for the capture of the smaller islands around Okinawa itself, where base facilities could be built to support the operation. All of this required an immense amount of administrative and logistical planning, and it was clear that the original invasion date of 1 March was unachievable. So, Operation *Iceberg* was delayed for a month, with its start, codenamed 'L-Day', being set for 1 April 1945.

This delay also allowed Operation *Iceberg* to fully involve the British Pacific Fleet. On 7 March, the BPF arrived at its forward base at Manus in the Admiralty Islands. The island, 170 miles off the coast of New Guinea, lay on the northern rim of the Bismarck Sea, 350 miles north-east of Japanese-held Rabaul. Once the fleet had been refuelled, it embarked

During Operation *Iceberg*, the BPF was under American command. Shown here aboard USS *Indianapolis* are Adm. Chester W. Nimitz, CinC US Pacific Fleet (left); Adm. Ernest J. King, CinC US Navy (centre) and V. Adm. Raymond A. Spruance, Commander of the US Fifth Fleet, to which the British force was attached. *Indianapolis* served as the Fifth Fleet flagship.

OPPOSITE TASK FORCE CRUISING FORMATION, OPERATION *ICEBERG*, 1945

For Operation *Iceberg*, the invasion of Okinawa, the BPF was under the overall control of the US Navy, now highly experienced in Pacific fast carrier operations. Several of their procedures were adopted including American standard cruising formations. This one, 'Cruising Disposition 5B' (CD 5B) was used by TF 57 for much of the air campaign. Designed to give the TF's four-fleet aircraft carriers the maximum possible space to operate, it allowed them to keep station within the TF, even when conducting air operations. It also reduced the risk of accidents when all four carriers were simultaneously launching or recovering aircraft, and made the most of the fleet's air defences to protect against kamikaze or bomber attack.

on a series of 'working up' exercises in readiness for serving alongside the US Navy. This participation though, was far from guaranteed. During their meeting in Hawaii in December 1944, Adm. Fraser and Adm. Nimitz had agreed that the British fleet would form its own separate Task Force, although it would serve as part of the US Fifth Fleet, commanded by V. Adm. Spruance.

To avoid causing any diplomatic discomfort, the American admiral wouldn't issue direct orders to the British admiral – instead he would send him 'requests', asking for Fraser's assistance in undertaking missions. This agreed, Fraser and his captains were raring to play their part in the main theatre of war. This though, didn't take into account Adm. Ernest J. King, the Commander-in-Chief of the US Navy (CINC USN) and its Chief of Operations. King had been adamant that the naval war in the Pacific should be an all-American affair and resented the political imposition of a Royal Naval presence in the theatre. He has been accused of being an ardent Anglophobe, but this may simply have been his own desire to prevent others sharing the US Navy's laurels in what appeared to be the final stages of the long, hard-fought naval campaign.

In this case, despite requests by Nimitz, King refused to ratify the attachment of the BPF to Spruance's command until 14 March, leaving Fraser and his men waiting in Manus for the request that never came. Even then, King attached a proviso to his approval. If required, the BPF could be withdrawn from the Fifth Fleet at a week's notice, if operational needs dictated it. What King had in mind was the sending of the BPF south, to support the Australian reconquest of Borneo rather than the American assault on Okinawa. What finally convinced King to use Fraser's fleet was the losses suffered by his own fleet off Iwo Jima.

Task Force 58 (TF 58), formerly the US Navy's Fast Carrier Task Force, formed the fighting core of the Fifth Fleet. Since January 1945 it had been commanded by V. Adm. Mitscher, who effectively rotated command of the force with the veteran fast carrier commander V. Adm. Halsey. It was composed of five carrier groups, each with three or four carriers, plus their escorts. TF 58 had been heavily involved in supporting the Iwo Jima invasion, and in a kamikaze attack on 21 February the carrier USS *Saratoga* had been badly damaged, and the escort carrier USS *Bismarck Sea* had been sunk. Still, TF 58 performed well, accounting for a total of 670 Japanese aircraft destroyed in the air or on the ground.

In early March, the Task Force was pulled back to the US naval base at Ulithi in the Caroline Islands for replenishment and repair. It was there, on 11 March, that another kamikaze strike badly damaged the carrier USS *Randolph*. So, with an escort carrier sunk and two damaged carriers sent back to the United States for repair, TF 58 was reorganized, and its five fast carrier groups were reduced to four. It was the damage to these carriers which finally convinced King that the British Pacific Fleet be used to reinforce Nimitz and Spruance. Both admirals had lobbied King extensively throughout early March, arguing the case that the BPF was a priceless asset for the Fifth Fleet, giving Spruance a powerful and flexible reserve, to support the American-led operation. In the end, King reluctantly acquiesced to the wishes of his fighting admirals, and so the Royal Navy was finally allowed to join its allies in time for the operation.

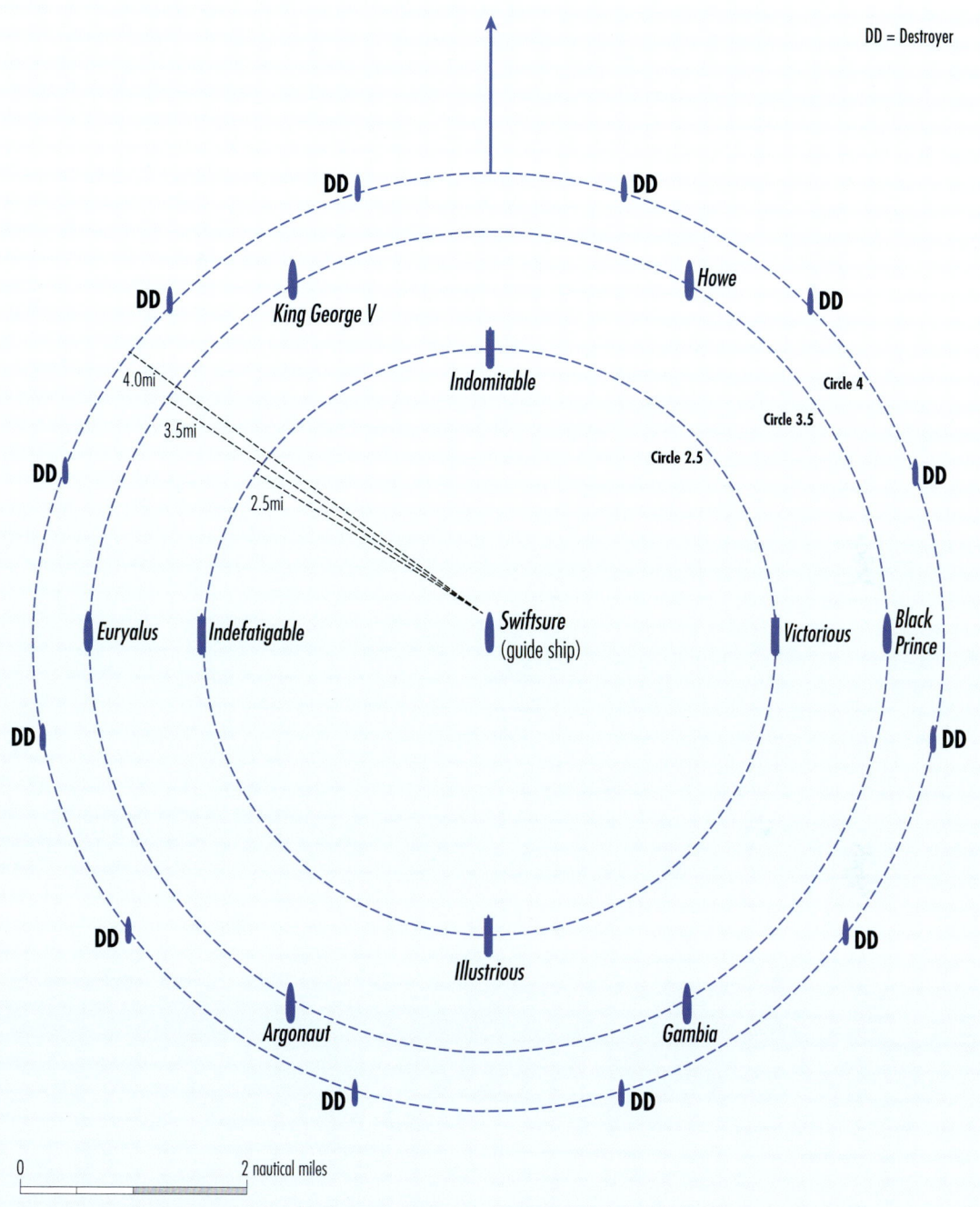

At the centre of the TF was the 'guide ship', a light cruiser, whose course dictated the axis and speed of the formation, according to orders issued from the fleet commander, Admiral Rawlings aboard his flagship HMS *King George V*. However, during active flying operations, control was ceded to Vice Admiral Vian, commander of the carrier strike force, whose flagship was the carrier HMS *Indomitable*. Once the guide ship changed course and speed, the rest of the TF would respond accordingly, to maintain the CD 5B formation. This was usually done when flying operations were being conducted, allowing the carriers to turn into the wind for flying aircraft off or landing them back on.

For defensive purposes, it was vital that the cruising disposition was maintained, whatever the circumstances. The carriers were dispersed in a diamond formation, ahead, astern and on the beam of the guide ship. They maintained a position on 'Circle 2.5', 2 ½ nautical miles from the guide ship. Vian's flagship was usually directly ahead of the guide ship. The second ring, 'Circle 3.5' was made up of the TF's battleships and cruisers, 3 ½ miles from the guide ship. They provided the main medium-range AA protection for the TF. The third ring, 'Circle 4' or 'Circle 4.5' was made up of fleet destroyers, providing anti-submarine as well as anti-aircraft protection.

Operation *Iceberg*

The aim of Operation *Iceberg* was the capture of the island of Okinawa, the largest island in the small Okinawa archipelago, which in turn formed part of the chain of Ryukyu Islands, which lay between the Pacific Ocean and the East China Sea.

The island's capture would place American aircraft within easy reach of the Japanese homeland. Ultimately, Okinawa would serve as a springboard for Operation *Olympic*, the Allied invasion of Japan. The assault on Okinawa itself would be an all-American operation, but, although the vast majority of the naval forces involved in Operation *Iceberg* were from the US Navy, it would now contain the British Pacific Fleet.

Throughout the American counter-attack in the Pacific it was considered vital that the enemy be given no respite between these 'island-hopping' assaults. So, on 14 March, while the US Marines were still 'mopping up' the last pockets of Japanese resistance on Iwo Jima, Task Force 58, the US fast carrier task force, sailed from Ulithi, bound for the seas around Okinawa. Although the Fifth Fleet was commanded by Adm. Spruance, he received his orders from Adm. Nimitz, Commander-in-Chief of the US Pacific Fleet (CINC PAC). So, the British Pacific Fleet's operational commander, V. Adm. Rawlings, would ultimately be under the orders of Nimitz. Adm. Nimitz also had the ability to direct other naval forces to support Spruance if required.

The intention was to keep the Task Force on station off the island throughout Operation *Iceberg*, which was predicted to last two to three months. This would be achieved through the support of replenishment groups, supply ships, maintenance ships and escort carriers used as ferries for aircraft replacements and parts. This spoke volumes about the ability of the US Navy to achieve this through the dramatic increase of their Fleet Train supporting the Task Force, and the experience of the crews in maintaining their ships and air groups while at sea. TF 58 of course, was merely part of the large armada being assembled for Operation *Iceberg*. As well as the BPF, soon to be redesignated Task Force 57 (TF 57), Spruance's Fifth Fleet consisted of several other key elements.

TF 51, led by V. Adm. Turner, was the assault force, made up of the assault transports and landing vessels which would transport the US Marines and US Army troops who would carry out the landing. They were supported by R. Adm. Blandy's TF 52, the amphibious support force, which included minesweepers and anti-submarine net-laying ships (Task Group 52.2) and a powerful Support Carrier Group (TF 52.1) of 18 escort carriers, whose aircraft would support the troops ashore. They were accompanied by a sizeable escort screen. Another four escort carriers would follow, transporting aircraft destined to be based ashore, once the island's airfields were captured. TF 52.1 was under the command of R. Adm. Durgin. TF 54,

Corsairs ranged on the after deck of HMS *Illustrious*, preparing for the formation's flying off. During Operation *Iceberg*, the veteran carrier had two squadrons of Corsairs embarked from 1830 and 1833 NAS.

commanded by R. Adm. Deyo, was the Gunfire Covering Force, made up of 10 battleships, 11 cruisers and numerous destroyers. They would constitute the naval bombardment force. TF 50 was comprised of the fleet's Support and Service units – the seaplane carriers, escort carriers, fleet oilers, logistics ships and other support vessels which made up the Fifth Fleet's sizeable supply train.

The British mission

The Sakishima Islands (Sakishima Guntō in Japanese) formed the south-westerly end of the Ryukyu island chain. The Sakishimas formed a chain of islands 100 miles long, with its most easterly island group, the Miyako Rettō, just 150 miles to the south-west of Okinawa, and 100 miles from V. Adm. Mitscher's US carriers. Apart from the outflung westerly small island of Yonakuni Jima (or Shima), 37 miles further west, the most westerly island group in the chain was the Yayeyama Rettō, clustered around the largest island in the Sakishima chain, Iriomote Jima. The two key islands though, were Ishigaki Island (Ishigaki Jima) to the east of Iriomote, and Miyako Island (Miyako Jima) in Miyako Rettō. Both islands contained three Japanese airfields, and these, the closest just 120 miles east of Japanese-held Formosa, would be ideal staging posts for Japanese kamikazes, sent there to launch attacks on the Allied armada.

Therefore, the mission given to the BPF was the neutralization of the airfields in the Sakishima Islands and to destroy any aircraft they encountered. This should greatly reduce the risk of extensive losses to the Fifth Fleet from kamikaze attacks. Adm. Nimitz certainly didn't underestimate the threat posed by Japanese kamikaze attacks. He was also aware that the most experienced Japanese pilots, including those prepared to pilot kamikaze planes, were those in China and Formosa. Those operating from the Japanese homeland were, for the most part much less experienced airmen. So, for Nimitz, the kamikaze threat posed from the south-west of Okinawa was greater than the one from the north.

Adm. Fraser in Sydney had wanted the British fleet to retain its identity within the larger American fleet, rather than be subsumed into the larger formation. This mission guaranteed that the BPF would retain its own structure, albeit rebranded as Task Force 57, and serving under Spruance's command. It helped too that the British would be operating to the south-west of the main American fleet, and would have their own distinct operational area. So, the task of subduing the Sakishimas, and protecting the western flank of the US Fifth Fleet was the ideal mission for the BPF. As TF 57 had been given a semi-independent role in Operation *Iceberg*, it allowed the Task Force to operate in its own way and to plan its attacks in a manner which best suited the abilities of its airmen and their aircraft. It also allowed the Fleet Air Arm crews to hone their skills and gain further experience on this important but secondary mission, before working more closely with the veteran American fast carrier group.

A Grumman Avenger of TF 57 being armed, in April 1945, before an attack on a Japanese airfield in the Sakishima Islands. These aircraft could carry up to 2,000lbs (907kg) of bombs. The usual payload was four of the 500lb. MC bombs pictured here.

Although the BPF had been designated a Task Force, it was really little more than a Task Group in strength, when compared to Adm. Mitscher's veteran Task Force 58 (Fast Carrier Force). Mitscher had 11 large fleet carriers and 6 light carriers in his TF 58, divided into four Task Groups, each of

OPPOSITE FLEET AIR ARM ATTACK METHODS, OPERATION *ICEBERG*, 1945

When attacking Japanese airfields in the Sakishima Islands, the FAA used three methods of attack. Their aim was to put the six airfields there out of action, to prevent them being used as staging posts for kamikaze attacks on the US Fifth Fleet off Okinawa. This was done by bombing and cratering the runways. On Miyako Jima, Higara airfield had two runways, Nobara two and Sukuma one, all paved using crushed coral. On Ishigaki Jima, only the two runways on Ishigaki Main airfield were paved, while Miyara and Hegina were single grass strips.

between three and five carriers. So, Rawlings' command of four British fleet carriers was comparable to one of these American groups. Also, on average, the US Navy's carrier groups had around 320 aircraft embarked, a mixture of dive bombers, torpedo bombers and fighters. R. Adm. Vian's 1st Carrier Squadron had just 235 aircraft embarked in its four carriers. This though, would increase to 290 aircraft with the arrival of HMS *Formidable*, which was still en route to the Far East. The smaller capacity of the British carriers was largely because of the smaller hangar space, which in turn was due to the armoured protection of the British carriers. However, this armour would prove its worth during the campaign.

It is worth noting that until this point in the war, the Royal Navy had tended to impose operational limits on its carriers and embarked squadrons. On all the carriers apart from *Indefatigable*, the usual limits of this 'operational tour' had been passed in February. Normally, the carriers would be sent to their home base for refit and repair and would sail again with fresh Air Wings embarked. In this case though, as the BPF was about to embark on a major operation in company with the US Navy, sending the carriers back to Sydney, over 2,000 miles away, was considered operationally unacceptable. So, the embarked aircraft and air crews would simply have to extend their operational tour until the carriers had completed their part in Operation *Iceberg*. This meant that the Fleet Air Arm air crews and the carriers' flight deck crews were all veterans of the Sumatra campaign of 1944–45, and the large-scale air attack on Palambang in January. So, despite the strain on men, aircraft and ships, Task Force 58 would go into action with combat veterans crewing and supporting its aircraft.

For its part, Mitscher's larger Task Group 58 had already performed a similar function to the British operation in February, as a prelude to the Iwo Jima invasion. Then, the Task Group's carriers had launched a series of long-range sweeps over the Japanese homeland islands of Kyushu and Shikoku, as well as the Japanese mainland island of Honshu, in the region south of Osaka. The aim was to reduce the Japanese ability to oppose the invasion of

Corsairs and Avengers undergoing maintenance and repair on the flight deck of HMS *Formidable* during Operation *Iceberg*. It was a challenge to keep these aircraft fully operational during this period of almost daily sorties against the Sakishima Islands.

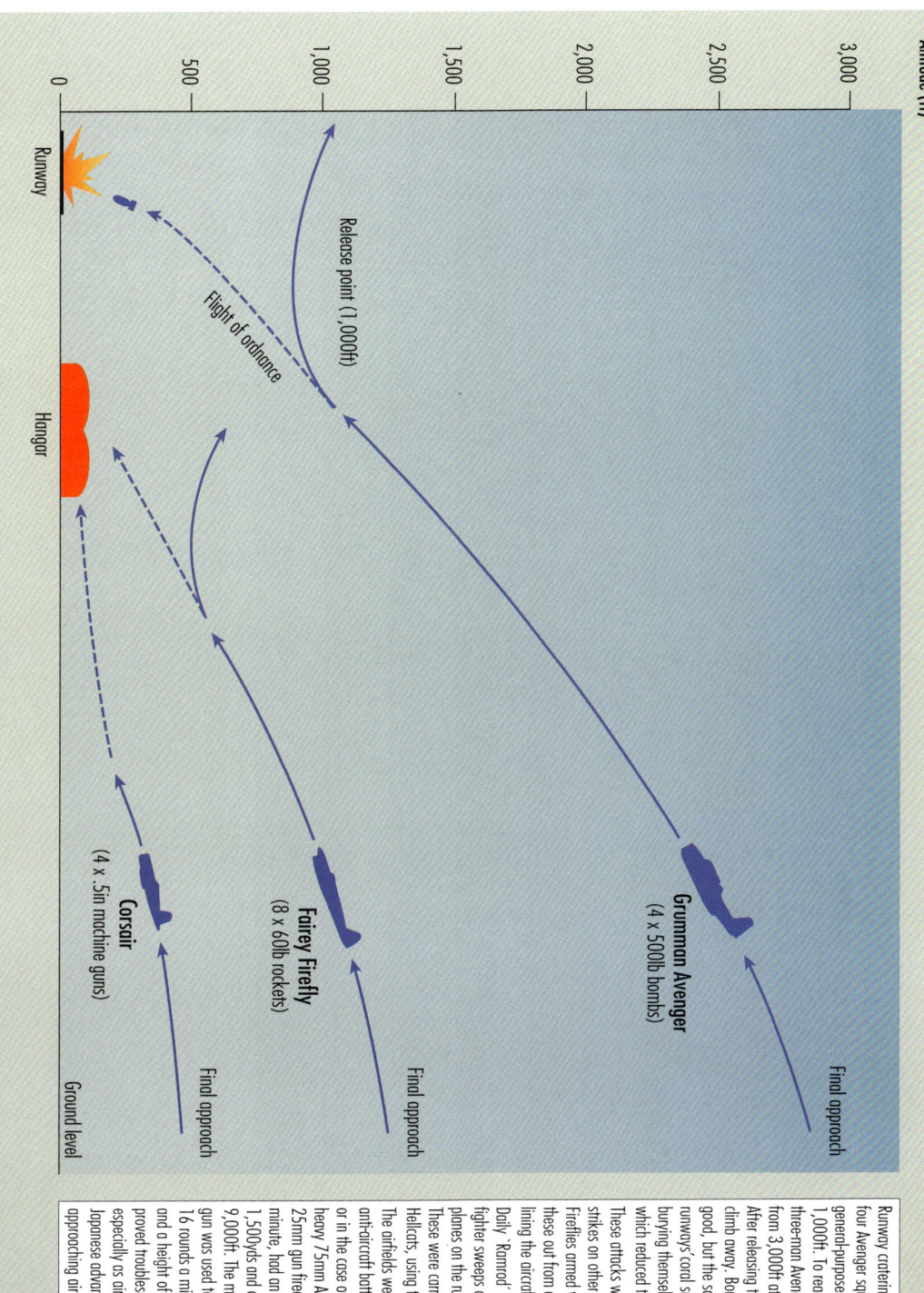

Runway cratering was carried out by the TF's four Avenger squadrons with four 500lb general-purpose bombs, dropped from 1,000ft. To reach its release point, the three-man Avenger made its final approach from 3,000ft at a dive angle of around 45°. After releasing the bombs, it would bank and climb away. Bombing accuracy was usually good, but the soft nature of some of the runways' coral surface led to bombs often burying themselves deep before exploding, which reduced the size of the crater.

These attacks were augmented by rocket strikes on other airfield facilities. Hellcats or Fireflies armed with 60lb rockets carried these out from a height of around 500ft by lining the aircraft up on the target.

Daily 'Ramrod' strikes were also made – fighter sweeps over the airfields, targeting planes on the runways or other targets. These were carried out by Corsairs or Hellcats, using their 0.5in machine guns.

The airfields were mostly protected by anti-aircraft batteries of light 25mm AA guns, or in the case of Ishigaro Main and Higara, heavy 75mm AA guns. The Type 96 twin 25mm gun fired around 120 rounds per minute, had an effective range of 1,500yds and could engage targets up to 9,000ft. The more potent Type 88 75mm gun was used to fire flack barrages of up to 16 rounds a minute, at a range of 5 miles and a height of up to 23,000ft. These both proved troublesome to the attackers, especially as air warning radar gave the Japanese advance warning of an approaching air strike.

Iwo Jima. This proved successful, with US naval airmen claiming over 280 enemy aircraft were destroyed. These attacks were repeated twice more, from 1 to 4 March and again ten days later, as a prelude to the Okinawa operation. These disruptive attacks were successful, despite minor damage to the carrier USS *Hancock* and a destroyer, the USS *Halsey Powell*, on 20 March.

The intention was to repeat the operation, this time in the Sakishima Islands, using the British carrier force. V. Adm. Mitscher's immensely powerful Carrier Strike Force, TG 58, began air strikes against the defences on Okinawa on 23 March, supported by the numerous escort carriers of TG 52.1. The delay in Adm. King authorizing the attachment of the BPF to Spruance's fleet influenced operations. TF 57 was due to arrive in its operational area on 23 March, the day the American air strikes began. Thanks to King's reluctance to involve the British, Rawlings' Task Force was delayed by two and a half days. As a result, it began its flying operations on 26 March. Meanwhile, as TF 57 steamed north towards the Sakishimas, Rear Adm. Vian's staff were busily studying intelligence reports and maps, to plan their air offensive against those key Japanese airfields.

Within the Sakishima chain, the airfields were concentrated on the two largest islands. On Ishigaki, the three airfields were called Ishigaki Main, Miyara and Hegina, while the three on Miyako were Hirara, Nobara and Sukuma. On Ishigaki, only Ishigaki Main had a paved runway – the other two were grass airfields. On Miyako though, all the airfields had paved runways, albeit ones built using crushed coral. In fact, at Hirara, the largest of the three, there were actually three paved runways on the site, while Nobara had two of them, and Sukuma only one. The largest airfields were well defended, with 92 guns emplaced around Ishigaki Main (26 heavy and 66 light AA guns), and 66 defending Hirara (12 heavy and 54 light). The two smaller secondary airfields on each island had between 10 and 16 light AA guns emplaced around them. So, with Japanese lookout stations able to give adequate warning of an attack, the British air strikes were likely to run into some heavy opposition.

The basic plan was simple. The British air strikes would crater the runways of the six airfields, and render them inoperable. The attacks would be repeated to foil any repair attempts, while bombs with delayed-action fuses would also discourage Japanese attempts to repair the damage. To prevent reinforcements from reaching the Sakishima Islands, a substantial CAP would be maintained over both Ishigaki Shima and Miyako Shima, as well

Fleet Air Arm air crew at a pre-strike briefing aboard their carrier. Here, they were given details of their objective, the attack on it and any other relevant information, gleaned in most cases from a reconnaissance conducted earlier that day. It is worth noting that many of these young men carry the 'wavy' shoulder stripes of the Royal Naval Volunteer Reserve (RNVR).

The bombing of Japanese airfields in the Sakishimas was a repetitive business. Once the airfields were put out of commission, the Japanese would repair them overnight, and so the attack would have to be repeated. However, this seemingly mundane task greatly reduced the exposure of the US Fifth Fleet to kamikaze attacks.

as over the Task Force itself. The only drawback was that both air strikes and CAP missions would be carried out in daylight, as at that point the Fleet Air Arm pilots lacked the training to land in the dark, while the carriers themselves also lacked the night-landing equipment they needed to make this a viable undertaking. Still, Vian and his staff were optimistic that their air strikes would achieve the objective of 'neutralizing' the Sakishima airfields, and so reduce the risk of kamikaze attacks to Spruance's fleet.

ORDER OF BATTLE

TASK FORCE 57 (THE BRITISH PACIFIC FLEET (BPF))
MARCH 1945
Commander-in-Chief (CINC): Adm. Sir Bruce Fraser (in Fleet Headquarters, Sydney)
Operational Task Force Commander: V. Adm. Sir Bernard Rawlings.
1st Carrier Aircraft Squadron (Task Group 57.2) R. Adm. Sir Philip Vian[1]
Indomitable (flagship) (Indomitable-class fleet aircraft carrier) Capt. Eccles
Illustrious (Illustrious-class fleet aircraft carrier) Capt. Lambe
Victorious (Illustrious-class fleet aircraft carrier) Capt. Denny
Indefatigable (Implacable-class fleet aircraft carrier) Capt. Graham
En-route from UK as reinforcement:
HMS *Formidable* (Illustrious-class fleet aircraft carrier) Capt. Ruck-Keene
1st Battle Squadron (Task Group 57.1) V. Adm. Sir Bernard Rawlings
King George V (fleet flagship) (King George V-class battleship) Capt. Halsey
Howe (King George V-class battleship) Capt. McCall
4th Cruiser Squadron (Task Group 57.4) R. Adm. Patrick 'Daddy' Brind
HMS *Swiftsure* (flagship) (Swiftsure-class light cruiser) Capt. McLaughlin

---

1   Vian held the acting rank of V. Adm. He was confirmed in the rank on 8 May 1945.

HMNZS Gambia (Fiji-class light cruiser) Capt. William-Powlett
HMCS *Uganda*.(Fiji-class light cruiser) Capt. Mainguy
Black Prince. (Bellona-class light cruiser) Capt. Lees
HMNZS *Achilles* (Leander-class light cruiser) Capt. Otway-Ruthven
Argonaut. (Dido-class anti-aircraft cruiser) Capt. McCarthy
Euryalus. (Dido-class anti-aircraft cruiser) Capt. Oliver-Bellasis
Destroyer Screen (Task Group 57.8) R. Adm. John Edelston (in Fleet HQ, Sydney)
25th Destroyer Flotilla Capt. Richard Onslow
HMS *Grenville* (G-, H- and I-class flotilla leader) Capt. Onslow
HMS *Ulster*, HMS *Undine*, HMS *Urania*, HMS *Undaunted* (S-, T-, U-, V- and W-class destroyers)
4th Destroyer Flotilla Cdr Philip Saumarez
HMAS *Quickmatch*, HMAS *Quiberon*, HMS *Queensborough* (flotilla leader), HMS *Quality* (Q- and R-class destroyers)
27th Destroyer Flotilla Cdr George Norfolk
HMS *Whelp* (flotilla leader), HMS *Wager* (S-, T-, U-, V- and W-class destroyers)
Fleet Train (Task Force 112) R. Adm. Douglas Fisher (HMS *Tyne*, at Eniwetok Atoll)
Escort Screen (Task Group 112.3) (all Royal Navy or Royal Australian Navy manned)
Acting Capt. Herbert Buchanan RAN
HMAS *Napier* (task group leader), HMAS *Nizam*, HMAS *Nepal*, HMAS *Norman* (J-, K- and N-class destroyers)
HMS *Crane*, HMS *Pheasant*, HMS *Woodcock*, HMS *Whimbrel* (Black Swan-class sloops)
HMS *Avon*, HMS *Findhorn*, HMS *Parret* (River-class frigates)
Escort Carrier Group (Task Group 112.2) (all Royal Navy manned) Capt. William Carne
Ferry Carriers (2):
HMS *Striker* Task Group flagship (Attacker-class escort aircraft carrier) Capt. Carne
HMS *Ruler* (Ameer-class escort aircraft carrier) Capt. Currey
Replenishment Carriers (2):
HMS *Slinger* (Ameer-class escort aircraft carrier) Capt. Moore
HMS *Speaker* (Ameer-class escort aircraft carrier) Capt. James
Replenishment and Support Group (Task Group 112.1)
Royal Navy manned:

Repair Ships (3):
Unicorn (Unicorn-class light aircraft carrier) – aircraft repair ship
Resource (Resource-class heavy repair ship)
Artifex (Artifex-class repair ship – converted merchantman)
Destroyer Depot Ship (1):
Tyne (Tyne-class destroyer depot ship) flagship, TF 112
Netlayer (1):
Guardian (Guardian-class netlayer)
Royal Fleet Auxiliary (RFA) manned
Replenishment Oilers (8): *Arndale*, *Cedardale*, *Dingledale* (Dale-class replenishment oilers)
Brown Ranger (Ranger-class tanker)
Merchant Navy manned
Victualling Store Ships (4): *City of Dieppe, Denbighshire, Fort Alabama*
Armament Store Ships (10): *Corinda, Darvel, Hermelin, Heron, Kheti, Pacheco, Prince de Liege, Princess Maria Pia, Robert Maersk, Thyra S.*
Air Store Ship (1): *Fort Colville*
Naval Store Ship (1): *Bacchus*
Distilling Ship (1): *Stagpool*
Hospital Ships (2): *Oxfordshire, Tjitalengka*
Oilers (4): *San Ambrosio, San Adolpho, Wave King, Aase Mersk*
Fleet Air Arm Air Groups
HMS *Indomitable* 857 NAS[2]
15 Grumman Avengers
(5th Fighter Wing) 1839 NAS 15 Grumman Hellcats
1844 NAS 14 Grumman Hellcats
HMS *Victorious* 849 NAS 14 Grumman Avengers
(47th Fighter Wing) 1834 NAS 19 Vought Corsairs
1836 NAS 18 Vought Corsairs
HMS *Indefatigable* 820 NAS
20 Grumman Avengers
(24th Fighter Wing) 887 NAS
20 Supermarine Seafires
894 NAS 20 Supermarine Seafires
1770 NAS 9 Fairey Fireflies
HMS *Illustrious* 854 NAS 16 Grumman Avengers
(15th Fighter Wing) 1830 NAS 18 Vought Corsairs
1833 NAS 18 Vought Corsairs
HMS *Formidable* 848 NAS 19 Grumman Avengers
(6th Fighter Wing) 1841 NAS 18 Vought Corsairs
1842 NAS 18 Vought Corsairs
Total: 84 Avenger torpedo bombers and 189 single-engine fighters (29 Hellcat, 109 Corsair, 40 Seafire and 9 Firefly fighters), for a total of 290 aircraft. In addition, *Victorious* had two Supermarine Walrus float planes embarked, for air-sea-rescue (ASR) duties.

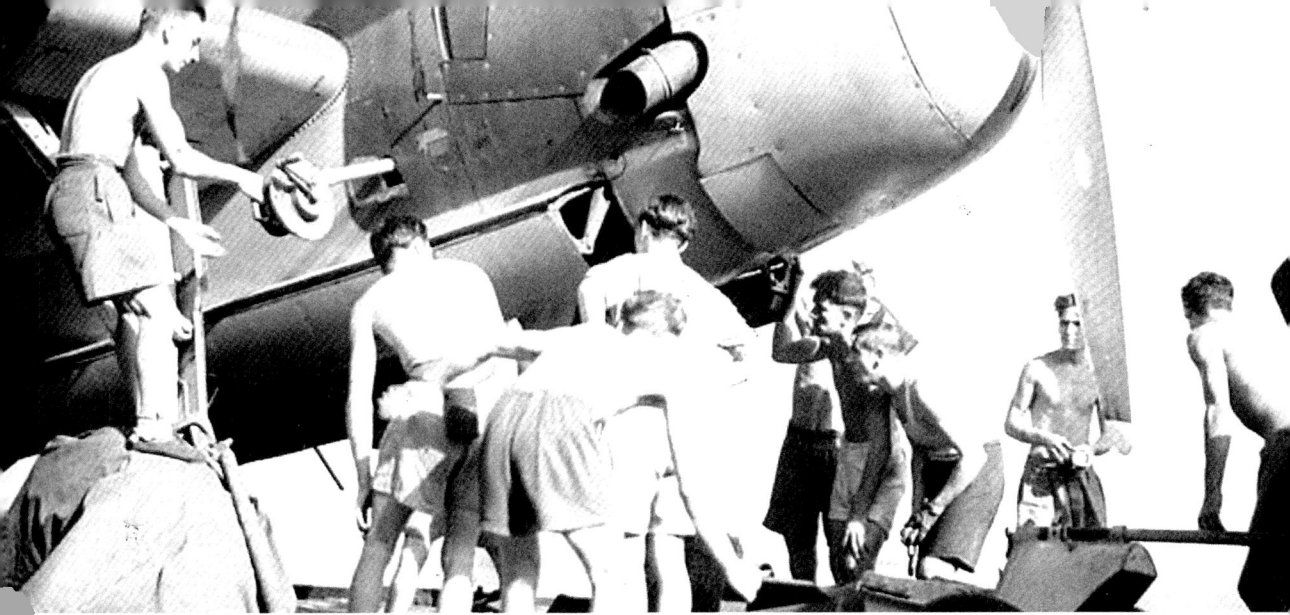

On the flight deck of *Illustrious,* an Avenger of 854 NAS is armed before a strike. The 16 Avengers that made up the squadron at the start of Operation *Iceberg* could carry up to four of these 500lb general-purpose (GP) bombs.

THE CAMPAIGN

Joining the US Fifth Fleet

On 15 March, while his flagship was on exercise off the British forward base at Manus, V. Adm. Rawlings received the order from Adm. Fraser in Sydney to take the fleet to sea, and to report to CINC PAC, Adm. Nimitz, for duties relating to Operation *Iceberg*. The invasion of Okinawa was scheduled to begin in just over two weeks. This order from Fraser, Commander-in-Chief of the British Pacific Fleet (CINC BPF), was the result of the formal request from Nimitz, sent at noon the day before, for the British to join his own fleet for this key operation. Essentially, the BPF was invited to serve as part of Adm. Spruance's US Fifth Fleet. Rawlings acknowledged the order, as the battleship returned to Manus. His signal to Nimitz read: 'I hereby report Task Forces 112 and 113 in accordance with orders received from C-in-C BPF. It is with a feeling of great pride and pleasure that the BPF joins the US naval forces under your command.' At long last the Royal Navy was about to fight alongside its American allies, during the final push towards the Japanese homeland.

All further exercises were cancelled as the fleet prepared to sail. Rawlings' staff, and those of his carrier commander, R. Adm. Vian, began a hectic round of planning and the issuing of orders, as the fleet prepared for departure. This planning included refuelling and resupply arrangements, in conjunction with the Fleet Train, suitable for three weeks of continuous operation in the Okinawa theatre. The organizers were encouraged when, on 16 March, they received an acknowledgement to Rawlings' signal from Adm. Nimitz. It read: 'The US Pacific Fleet welcomes the British Carrier Task Force and attached units, which will greatly add to our power to strike the enemy and will also show our unity of purpose in the war against Japan.'

Meanwhile, the ships of the fleet took on last-minute fuel and stores, which was always something of a struggle in such an open anchorage amid a heavy swell. Meanwhile Vian and his staff made sure that all four of his fleet carriers were as well equipped as they could possibly be and had something close to their full complement of aircraft and airmen. On 17 March, the fleet tankers and their escorts left Manus and headed towards their pre-arranged refuelling positions in the Philippine Sea, 1,000 miles to the north.

OPPOSITE TASK FORCE 57 OPERATING AREA, MARCH – MAY, 1945

Adm. Sir Bruce Fraser (1888–1981) commanded the BPF from its inception. However, for Operation *Iceberg* he remained at his headquarters in Sydney, and his deputy, V. Adm. Rawlings, assumed operational command of the fleet. This freed Fraser to concentrate on the fleet's liaison with the US Navy, and to coordinate the complex logistical support arrangements for TF 57.

They were accompanied by two of the Fleet Train's escort carriers, used to transport replacement aircraft, and fighters to provide air cover during refuelling operations.

Finally, at 0830hrs on 18 March, Rawlings' flagship *King George V* put to sea, accompanied by *Howe*, three cruisers and five destroyers. Instead of heading straight towards Okinawa, the fleet would sail to an intermediary port of call, a little under halfway to its operational area near Okinawa. Ulithi Atoll in the Caroline Islands, midway between Guam and Palau, was the forward base of the US Fifth Fleet. There, Rawlings would refuel and receive last-minute orders and intelligence reports before leading his fleet further north. The atoll lay 840 miles to the north-west of Manus, the equivalent of just under two days of sailing. So, arrival there was expected around dawn on 20 March. Vian's carrier squadron was delayed slightly, as poor weather prevented the transfer of the last of its replacement aircraft and stores. The four carriers finally left Manus at 1100hrs, escorted by six destroyers. Two cruisers and a destroyer still remained in port, undergoing repairs or refits, and would follow on as soon as they were able.

Rawlings and his superior, Adm. Fraser in Sydney, had been briefed on the planning for Operation *Iceberg* – the invasion of Okinawa – and so had a fair idea of what lay ahead. During the two-day transit from Manus to Ulithi the British warships conducted exercises. Then, at 0930hrs on 20 March, *King George V* entered Ulithi's anchorage, followed a few hours later by Vian's carriers. Once at anchor, the British ships began refuelling and taking on stores, ready for the next leg of their voyage. This was the Royal Navy's first experience of using its American counterparts' logistical support in the Pacific theatre. It was hugely impressed. It helped of course, that the anchorage was virtually empty. The bulk of Spruance's Fifth Fleet, including Task Force 58 – the carrier strike force – had sailed from Ulithi on 14 March, the day before Rawlings received his orders to join the offensive.

The anchorage though, was still on high alert. Just nine days before, on 11 March, in an operation codenamed *Tan 2*, 24 Japanese Yokosuka P1Y 'Ginga' twin-engined medium bombers had taken off from Kanoya on Kyushu in Japan, and headed towards Ulithi. Due to navigational and technical problems only two of these land-based bombers (codenamed 'Frances' by the Allies) had reached their destination after the 1,500 mile flight. One had crashed on the edge of the atoll, but the second had penetrated the base's defences, and carried out a kamikaze attack on the carrier USS *Randolph*. The bomber struck the carrier's stern and blew up next to where 200 crewmen were watching a film on the hangar deck. In all, 27 of these men were killed and over a hundred wounded. The damaged *Randolph* was still in the lagoon when the British fleet arrived. It was repaired there and rejoined the fleet the following month.

The refuelling continued over the days that followed the British arrival, despite poor weather and a troublesome swell within the anchorage. This was carried out by US naval tankers and warships. On the morning of Thursday 22 March, a seaplane arrived from Nimitz's headquarters on Guam bearing CINC PAC's Chief-of-Staff, V. Adm. Morris, who discussed modifications to the Operation *Iceberg* plans with Adm. Rawlings, and reiterated the British role in the coming offensive. Nimitz himself had planned to come, but had to bow

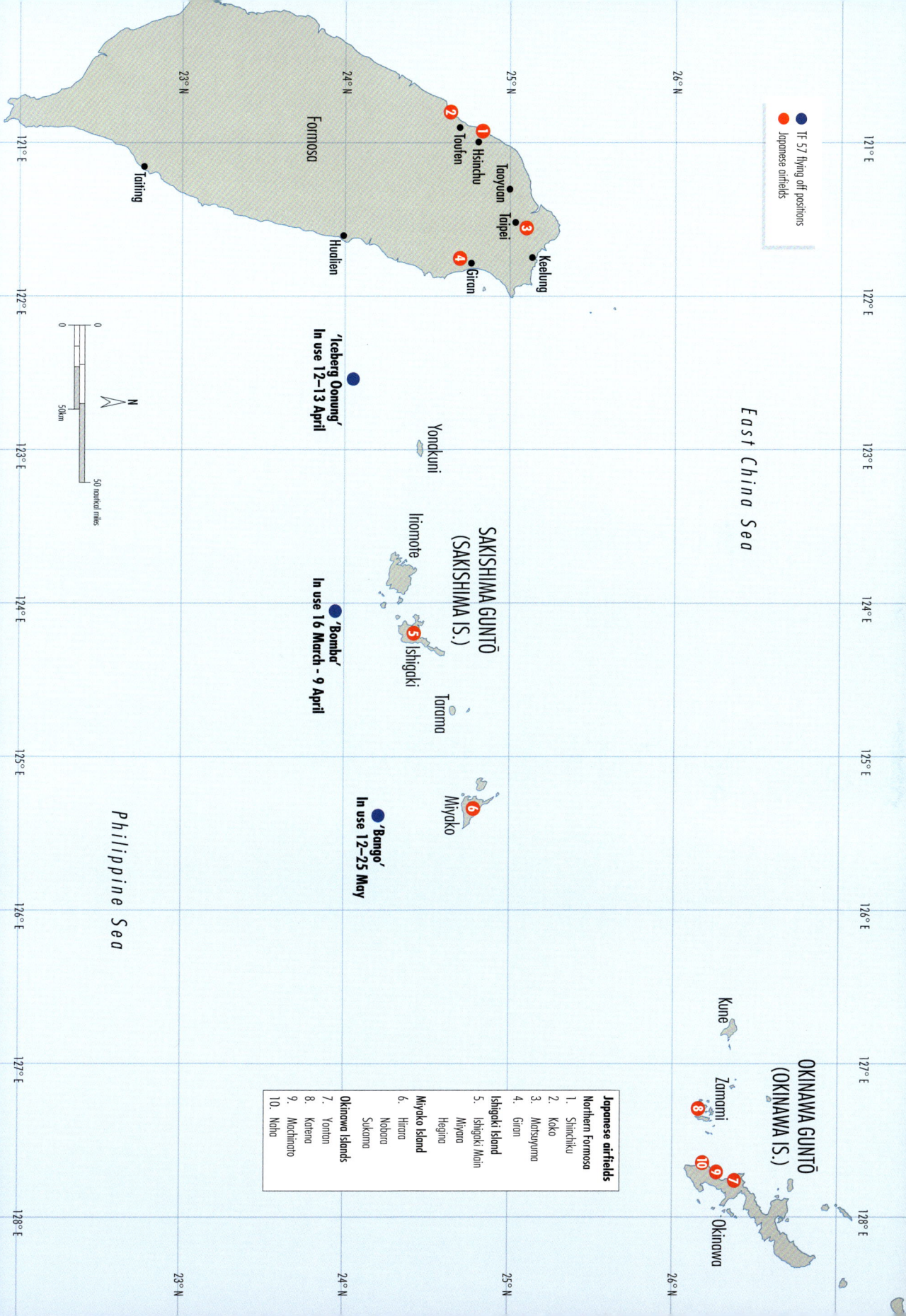

out due to a cold. This led to a frenzied day of activity by Rawlings and his staff, as final detailed orders were circulated around the fleet. The intention was to have everything ready for a departure the following morning.

Sure enough, at 0630hrs on Friday morning, the British fleet sailed from Ulithi, and set a course for the Sakishima Islands. It was at that point, on leaving Ulithi, that the BPF was rebranded. From that point on, it was officially known as 'Task Force 57 (British Carrier Force)', a part of the US Fifth Fleet. Rawlings' flagship, together with *Howe*, were designated Task Unit 1 (TU 1), while Vian's carrier squadron became Task Unit 2 (TU 2). The cruisers, led temporarily by *Euryalus*, became TU 5 and the destroyers TU 8. The crews were keyed up, well aware that soon they would be rejoining battle with the Japanese. This time though, rather than operating off Sumatra, they would be attacking the enemy in its own territory, the southern tip of the Japanese archipelago, which stretched northwards towards the heart of the Japanese homeland.

The first attacks

It was just over 1,000 miles from Ulithi to the Task Force's flying-off point, 100 miles due south of Miyako Jima, at the north-eastern end of the Sakishima chain. So, just before dawn on Sunday 25 March, at 0600hrs, Rawlings' TF 57 rendezvoused with the Logistics Support Group (TG 112.2) and began refuelling at sea. The refuelling tankers *San Ambrosio*, *Cedardale* and *San Alfonso* (designated TG 112.2.1) had left Manus on 17 March, escorted by two sloops and a frigate. Two days later, the escort carriers *Striker* and *Speaker* followed them (as TG 112.2.2), escorted by the destroyers *Kempenfelt* and *Whirlwind*. The rendezvous at Rendezvous Point Ant (18° 30' North, 129° 22' East) went smoothly, and operations began when four replacement Avengers were flown off from *Striker*, and landed on *Victorious* and *Indomitable*, to replace aircraft damaged during exercises off Ulithi.

V. Adm. Bernard Rawlings (1889–1962) held full operational control of TF 57 during the Okinawa campaign, flying his flag in the battleship HMS *King George V*. A veteran of the war in the Mediterranean, Rawlings proved a skilled and professional commander, who was able to foster an excellent working relationship with his US counterparts.

Striker was the flagship of Commodore Carne's 30th Aircraft Carrier Squadron (30 ACS), a rather grand title for the handful of escort carriers attached to the Fleet Train, to ferry replacement aircraft, to replenish warships and to provide maintenance and repair facilities to TF 57 when it was deployed on operations. Meanwhile *Speaker* flew off her Hellcats from 1840 Naval Air Squadron (NAS) to provide a CAP screen during the replenishment that followed. At the same time, six Avengers flown off from the Task Force fleet carriers carried out anti-submarine patrols around the assembly of ships. Low cloud prevented the combined anti-aircraft exercises planned by the fleet, but Hellcats towing windsock-like drogues allowed the capital ships some target practice. During this practice, when 2pdr 'pom-pom' rounds from *Indomitable* almost struck the battleship *Howe*, Capt. Eccles had to signal his apologies.

Meanwhile, as the three tankers concentrated on the capital ships and cruisers, *Striker* refuelled the fleet's destroyers, including her own two escorts. At first everything went smoothly, but the long Pacific swell increased as the morning wore on, and the line-astern method of refuelling proved increasingly problematic when refuelling the battleships and fleet carriers. Fortunately, all the warships had refuelled before leaving Ulithi, and all that was required that Sunday was a topping up. Then at noon, the Tanker Group (TG 112.2.1) and the Escort Carrier Group (TG 112.2.2) withdrew, leaving Rawlings' warships to continue northwards to their flying-off point, 360 miles or 18 hours steaming to the north-west.

Rendezvous Area Ant was established by Rawlings before the start of Operation *Iceberg*, and would only be used once. Another three rendezvous areas, codenamed 'Cootie', 'Midge'

The flight deck of a British armoured carrier had two lifts, one forward and one aft, so assembling aircraft for a sortie or returning them to the hangars on their return involved a lot of work by the flight deck crew, seen here lined up for inspection. During flying operations, these specialists were responsible for making sure everything worked smoothly. In this picture taken aboard HMS *Indefatigable* in early April 1945, a Supermarine Seafire is being ranged aft from the forward lift, ready for a sortie. In the background, Avengers of 820 NAS are being readied for take-off.

and 'Mosquito' were located between 250 and 350 miles south of the Sakishima Islands, with Cootie being the closest, and Midge the furthest away. By rotating these points, there was less chance that the Japanese would discover where they were. The next replenishment was to be in five days, at Rendezvous Area Midge.

Day 1: Monday 26 March

At 0600hrs on Monday 26 March, half an hour before dawn, Task Force 57 arrived in its operating area, Flying-off Point 'Bango', 100 miles south of Miyako Island. The previous evening, aboard *King George V*, V. Adm. Rawlings ceded tactical command to R. Adm. Vian, the commander of the carrier group. The idea behind this was that while aircraft were

HMS *Illustrious*, or 'Lusty', was an old warhorse, having launched the naval air strike on Taranto in November 1941, which crippled the Italian battlefleet. However, two months later, *Illustrious* was seriously damaged by Luftwaffe bombs. After repairs in the United States, the carrier saw further action in the Atlantic, the Mediterranean and the Indian Ocean, before joining TF 57. By April 1945, *Illustrious* was suffering from mechanical problems resulting from her old battle damage, and so the carrier was replaced by her sister ship, HMS *Formidable*, for the final phase of Operation *Iceberg*.

operating from the carriers, the commander of the carrier group was given tactical control of the fleet, so he could better control flying operations. It was important that both the carriers and the rest of the fleet surrounding them would coordinate their manoeuvres, such as turning into the wind to launch and recover aircraft, or to avoid approaching kamikaze waves. So, it was Vian aboard *Indomitable* who would remain in charge of the fleet until all of his aircraft had returned.

Five minutes later, at 0605hrs, Vian gave orders for the carriers to turn into the wind, and the day's flying operations began. The fleet had already deployed into formation, Cruising Disposition 5B, in line with US Navy practice. That morning, the guide ship in the centre of the formation was the cruiser *Swiftsure*, with *Indomitable* ahead of her, *Victorious* to port, *Illustrious* to starboard and *Indefatigable* following astern. The rest of the Task Group was arrayed around them. Operations began at 0615hrs, which began with the launch of a CAP screen over the Task Force. This was made up of 16 Seafires from 887 and 894 NAS, operating from *Indefatigable*. At the same time, a total of 48 Corsair fighters were launched from *Victorious* and *Illustrious*, drawn from 1830, 1833, 1834 and 1836 NAS.

Their mission was to strafe the airfields on Ishigaki and Miyako, destroying any Japanese aircraft encountered on the ground there, and to prevent any of them from taking off to attack the fleet. The Fleet Air Arm described these airfield strafing attacks as 'Ramrod' missions. Flying time to the islands was around 25–30 minutes. So, by 0645hrs the aircraft began reaching their targets. Sub. Lt Chute from 1836 NAS described the attack:

> A low level approach was made until nearing Miyako Jima when the sweep climbed up to 8000ft and swept round to an up-sun position of Hirara airfield. Drop tanks were released and Green Flight followed Red Flight in a steep diving attack on the airfield from the north-east, opening fire at long range and closing to zero feet where it could be seen that the targets attacked were either dummies or damaged aircraft.

HMS *Victorious* was a veteran of American fast carrier operations, having served with the US fleet in 1943. Ranged on the flight deck are the Corsairs of 1834 and 1836 NAS and her strike arm, the Avengers of 849 NAS. The carrier also had two Supermarine Walrus floatplanes embarked for air-sea-rescue (ASR) missions.

One Corsair ditched shortly after take-off, and the pilot was rescued by a Walrus 'before he had time to get his feet wet'.

This mission completed, it was time for the main event. This would be a bombing attack on the airfields and military facilities in the Sakishima chain, carried out by the carrier group's Avengers. There would be four strikes in all, each made up of a varying number of bombers, with Corsairs flying as their close escorts. Strike Able involved bombing attacks on barracks and AA defences at Ishigaki Main and Hegina. Strike Baker would attack three targets in the northern end of Miyako: the airfield buildings and barracks at Hirara and Nobara and a factory at Tomari in the centre of the island. These were preliminary strikes, undertaken at around 0645hrs that morning. The main attack, Strike Charlie, would form up over the Task Force at 0920hrs, before splitting into two waves – one heading to Ishigaki Main and the other to Hirara. Flying time to both islands was around 30 minutes; 857 NAS from *Indomitable* and 849 NAS from *Victorious* would target Ishigaki Main and 854 NAS from *Illustrious* would attack Hirara airfield on Miyako, as would 820 NAS from *Indefatigable*.

In all, Strike Charlie involved 40 Avengers, drawn from the four carriers, escorted by 24 Corsairs and 15 Hellcats, which would form top-cover, middle-cover and close-cover formations. Roughly half of the Strike Charlie force would attack each airfield. The attack was timed to reach them simultaneously, at 1000hrs. As the airmen of the first two strikes discovered, the airfields were extremely well defended. With 26 heavy (75mm) and 66 light AA (20mm and 25mm) guns at Ishigaki Main and 12 heavy and 54 light AA guns at Hirara, it was little wonder the attackers flew into a wall of accurately aimed AA fire. It didn't help that the defenders had been forewarned too, by the earlier air attacks. In all, three Avengers and a Corsair were shot down, two aircraft over each airfield; at Ishigaki, an Avenger from 854 NAS and a Corsair from 1836 NAS.

The latter was flown by Lt Cdr Tomkinson, commanding officer of 1836 NAS, who ditched in the sea after being shot down. He was trapped inside the cockpit as the fighter sank. Later, Capt. Denny of *Victorious* wrote: 'The loss of Lt. Cdr. Tomkinson RNVR is thought to have been caused by a faulty lifejacket. He was observed in his lifejacket in sight of land, and the position was accurately fixed. Sub Lt. Rhodes saw him in the sea and took part in the search.' Tomkinson was never found. Still, both airfields were heavily bombed, and some damage was caused. However, the crushed coral surfacing offered far too little resistance for the attackers' usually deadly 500lb MC bombs. Afterwards, one Avenger crewman claimed, 'We would have been better off using three-cornered tin tacks instead of bombs designed to sink the *Tirpitz*. They just went in, made a small hole and the Japs filled them in again that night.' Essentially, they smashed through the paved coral surface of the runway, and then buried themselves in the sand beneath it, without exploding.

Once the bombing runs were completed, the Hellcat fighter-bombers from 1839 and 1844 NAS, flying from *Indomitable* would end the strike with their own rockets on the Ishigaki and Hirara airport facilities, such as fuel dumps, control towers and maintenance sheds. That was scheduled to take place at 1020hrs. Each Hellcat carried six 5in rockets, three under each wing, and the airmen nicknamed them 'Holy Moses' for a reason. This brief rocket assault was spectacular, with 80–90 rockets striking each of the two airfields. These probably caused damage, but the results were hard to verify.

In fact, the same was probably true of the Avenger bombing runs. Afterwards, photographic reconnaissance by specially adapted Corsairs suggested that by the end of Monday, a total

Seafires ranged awaiting the flying-off signal. During Operation *Iceberg*, the Seafires of 887 and 894 NAS embarked in HMS *Indefatigable* formed the core of TF 57's CAP screen. These fighters lacked the range to escort air strikes, so this was the best use for them.

of 23 enemy aircraft had been attacked and destroyed on the ground. However, of these, 12 were judged to be genuine aircraft, while the remainder of the destroyed aircraft were dummies, made from wood and canvas. These 12 kills had to be balanced against the three British losses, with two pilots missing or killed. Another five aircraft suffered various forms of mechanical failure, but they managed to return to their carriers. It was a fairly high cost to pay for such a relatively small reduction to the kamikaze threat posed by the Japanese aircraft.

Throughout the day, the CAP screen over TF 57 had been doing its job well, with the Seafires from *Indefatigable* patrolling, then returning to refuel, while others took their place aloft. The only sign of the Japanese was a single twin-engined Mitsubishi Ki-46 'Dinah' aircraft on a reconnaissance sweep. It spotted the Task Force before being driven off by the patrolling Seafires. It was intercepted, but it managed to evade its pursuer without being shot down. Around noon, radar plotters thought a formation of Japanese bombers was approaching the Task Force, but they turned out to be B-24 Liberator bombers, operated by the US Navy, on an anti-submarine sweep over the Philippine Sea. For some reason they hadn't activated their IFF (identification, friend or foe) beacons, and once they wandered into the British area of operations they were fortunate not to have been attacked.

A destroyer on the outer screen of the Task Force fired at an approaching bomber, before it was identified as an American Liberator. After that, Vian ordered his CAP pilots and all escort crews to obtain visual recognition of the 'bogey' – the potential enemy contact on radar – before engaging it. Fortunately for the British, the Japanese didn't launch a major attack that day after their reconnaissance plane located the British Task Force. If they had, then the restrictive need to obtain visual recognition would have handed the initiative over to the attackers, and placed the CAP screen pilots at a disadvantage in a dogfight. By mid-afternoon, all of the strike aircraft and their escorts had landed back on their carriers. With flying operations over for the day, apart from the continued CAP screen provided by *Indefatigable*, Rawlings resumed tactical command of TF 57.

At 1530hrs, Rawlings turned the Task Force around to the south-east and withdrew to the assigned holding area, some 100 miles from the morning's flying-off point. This would set the pattern for the days to come – after a full day of air attacks, the Task Force would pull out of easy reach of the Sakishima chain for the night. Then it would return to its new flying-off point by dawn the following morning. It was a calm, clear night, with bright moonlight over the sea. This rendered the fleet vulnerable, but no enemy attack materialized. However, at 0245hrs on Tuesday morning, the American SM-1 air warning radar set in *Indomitable* detected a bogey approaching to the north. It was probably there to shadow the fleet during the night. A Hellcat was sent up to intercept it, but after being vectored in it found no sign of the bogey, which had flown into the clouds and made its escape. The incident may have been uneventful, but it underlined the fact that the Japanese knew where the British Task Force was, and so an attack on it could be expected.

Day 2: 27 March

The skies remained somewhat overcast, but at dawn on Tuesday 27 March, the Task Force was at Flying-off Point Bomba, 100 miles south of Ishigaki. At 0630hrs, just as the sun appeared, a Ramrod group of 24 Corsairs and Hellcats took off, bound for Iriomote Main and Hirara. As before, this was followed by Avenger strikes against all six airfields, with the Hellcats accompanying the strikes as top cover then peeling off to repeat the previous day's rocket attacks on the two main airfields, as well as other selected targets, such as barracks, aircraft dispersal bays and suspected wireless direction-finding stations. The Fireflies of 1770 NAS from *Indefatigable* joined in these attacks too. Although no Japanese aircraft were encountered in the air, the AA fire was as heavy as the day before. This time, two aircraft were lost, an Avenger crashlanding in the sea after being hit by AA fire over Hirara and a Corsair shot down over Ishigaki, and its pilot killed.

Supermarine Seafires of 887 and 894 NAS, preparing for take-off from HMS *Indefatigable*, at the start of another large-scale CAP sortie during Operation *Iceberg*. Due to their shorter range compared with the Corsairs embarked in the other carriers, it made sense to employ the Seafires in defence of the Task Force.

Sub. Lt Leonard of *Victorious* saw the Corsair go down: 'I strafed dummy aircraft and AA positions. Sub Lieutenant Spreckly from *Victorious* was flying on my port side, in line abreast, and was apparently hit by AA fire. He nosed over from 50 feet, hit the ground and exploded. After the first few days the Jap gunners stopped using tracer bullets and as we couldn't see them firing, up went our casualties.' Two more Seafires from the CAP patrol also crashed while landing on *Indefatigable*'s flight deck, and both pilots were killed. Six more aircraft were deemed inoperable due to mechanical failure, but all of these could be repaired.

The Avenger shot down over Miyako Jima was piloted by Lt Cdr Nottingham, the commanding officer of 854 NAS, embarked in *Illustrious*. The starboard wing of the South African's bomber was hit as he approached Hirara, and the plane caught fire. Nottingham ditched his bombs and banked away towards the sea. This proved too much for his damaged wing, which sheared off, and the Avenger began spiralling down from 3,000ft towards the sea. He ordered his two crewmen to bail out, but both were killed when the plane struck the sea. Nottingham survived and swam free, then remained floating in the sea to the south of Miyako Jima. The destroyer *Undine* was sent to look for him, but found an American airman instead, shot down three days earlier. It wasn't until the evening that ASR submarine USS *Kingfish* found Nottingham and took him aboard the boat. During the campaign, the presence of these ASR submarines would be a great reassurance to the British airmen.

More air strikes had been planned for Wednesday 28 March, but on Tuesday evening Rawlings decided to cancel them. In a report to Fraser, he gave two reasons. First, with the amphibious assault on Okinawa ('L-Day') scheduled to begin on Sunday 1 April, he wanted to make sure that TF 57 was back on station off the Sakishima Islands before the attack began. That way he could be sure to intercept any kamikazes attacking the American fleet from that direction. Secondly, according to weather reports from the US meteorological station in Guam, a tropical storm was expected to sweep westwards through the centre of the Philippine Sea around the same date, and it was felt it might develop into a typhoon. Rawlings wanted to complete the refuelling well before the weather deteriorated. In fact, this storm abated prior to reaching the area in which TF 57 was operating. So, Rawlings gave

The primary British bomb used by the Carrier Strike Force's Avengers off the Sakishima Islands was the 500lb General Purpose MC (medium capacity) bomb. However, it proved too powerful for the coral-paved runways of the Sakishima airfields, as these bombs usually buried themselves before exploding, which reduced the size of the crater in the runway caused by the explosion.

the order to break off his attacks a day early and head to Rendezvous Area Midge, where the Fleet Train's tankers would be waiting for him.

To fill the void left by TF 57, TG 52.1.1, R. Adm. Sprague's seven escort carriers from the Support Carrier Group (TF 52), moved west from their positions closer to Okinawa, and for two days they carried out their own air attacks on the Sakishima airfields using their Avenger bombers, supported by Wildcat fighters and Hellcat fighter-bombers. However, these attacks had little impact on the Japanese airfields. At 0730hrs on Wednesday morning, TF 57 rendezvoused with the waiting tankers in Midge. Replenishment proved a long and troublesome business, plagued by breakdowns of pumps and machinery, broken fuel lines and couplings, slow pumping rates and a succession of mistakes in either procedure or shiphandling. It didn't help that on Wednesday morning the fleet used an improvised British system, where half the fleet refuelled and reprovisioned, while the other half circled outside the rendezvous area waiting its turn. The technique was quietly abandoned, and from that point on TF 57 adopted US naval methods.

As well as fuel oil, Vian's carriers also replenished their stocks of aviation fuel (avgas). The whole process was much slower than expected, largely because the British tankers, all vessels which had been pressed into service rather than being custom-built for fleet service, pumped fuel at a much slower rate than their American counterparts. Not only did Rawlings vow to switch to American methods next time, but he also signalled Fraser in Sydney, asking him to source better and wider hoses and couplings to speed up refuelling next time. In the end, it was 1600hrs on Friday 30 March before the fleet refuelling had been completed. Throughout this, Hellcats from the escort carrier *Speaker* flew CAP missions over the fleet as it refuelled, while the escort carrier *Striker* flew off 17 aircraft, to replace the losses suffered by the Task Force off the Sakishima Islands.

L-Day

Both Rawlings and Vian were well aware that the US landing ships were approaching Okinawa. So, denying the Sakishima airfields to Japanese kamikaze groups was of crucial importance. So, at dawn on Saturday 31 March (L-1), the British resumed its air strikes against the Sakishima airfields. Setting the pattern for all subsequent air strikes, these were preceded by a reconnaissance, carried out by the two Air Group commanders, Lt Col. Hay of the Royal Marines and Cdr Luard. Both took off from the flagship well before dawn in a pair of Hellcats, and then split up, one fighter heading for each of the two target islands. It was Hay and Luard who would decide which targets would be attacked that morning. By this time, it was clear that the smaller fields, Miyara and Hegina on Ishigaki and Sakuma and Nobara on Miyako, didn't have any Japanese aircraft. It looked like they were there to accommodate reinforcements sent from Formosa, or acted as emergency landing strips.

As in the previous attacks, the British concentrated their efforts on the two main airfields, Ishigaki Main and Hirara. At 0630hrs, two Corsair Ramrod groups took off, each of 16 aircraft. After forming up over the Task Force, each one headed west, before shaping separate

The amphibious landing on Okinawa began on 'L-Day', Easter Sunday, 1 April. The initial assault was covered by an immense naval bombardment and numerous air strikes. By the end of the day, the US Army and US Marine Corps had established a viable beachhead spanning the centre of the narrow 'dogbone-shaped' island.

courses towards these main airfields. They shot up anything they could find, such as parked aircraft and ammunition and fuel dumps. An hour later, they were followed by the main bomber strikes, with both airfields targeted by a strike of 11 bomb-carrying Avengers. Each strike was escorted by a similar number of Hellcats, which, as before, were armed with rockets for opportunity rocket runs on airfield facilities. This time, the bombs had been modified to explode on contact with the ground, which should, in theory, cause more damage to the runways. While the paved runways were the primary targets, one flight of Avengers in each strike was ordered to concentrate on hangars, barracks and other airfield installations.

For the attacks that morning, the British had adopted an American security measure. A cruiser equipped with a powerful air search radar, in this case *Argonaut* accompanied by the destroyer *Wager* were stationed 30 miles to the west-north-west of the Task Force, on a bearing of 300°. The cruiser served as a radar picket as well as a diversion and had its own strong CAP screen circling over it. The Americans had found that the Japanese had learned to follow returning strikes, which told them where the attacking carriers were. So, the returning British strikes headed for *Argonaut*, where the aircraft were 'deloused' by checking that no Japanese aircraft were following them. The strikes then turned east towards their carriers. It was a very simple idea, and it was quickly adopted by the BPF for all subsequent strikes. The air search radar also had an additional use, in that it could detect where aircraft had ditched and vector the ASR submarine towards the site to rescue the aircrew. *Argonaut* and *Wager* rejoined the fleet in the late afternoon.

The two attacks were a success, and all but one of the planes returned safely. An Avenger of 854 NAS was hit during the attack on Iriomote, and it ditched in the sea to the south-east of the island. Fortunately for the crew, the ASR submarine, USS *Kingfish*, was on hand and was able to rescue all three crewmen. Two other aircraft, a Corsair and a Seafire, were badly damaged on landing. The Corsair was repairable, but the Seafire had to be written off and ditched over the side. A continuous CAP of Corsair fighters was maintained over the islands during daylight to discourage any Japanese response, while a CAP by Seafire fighters was maintained over the fleet. Due to their limited endurance, the Seafires were proving of little use in supporting the main air strikes, or providing CAP over the islands, so they were used solely for the protection of the fleet. Even then, the flight deck of *Indefatigable* was kept busy, as the Seafires of 887 and 894 NAS were regularly landing, refuelling and then taking off again.

At dusk, around 1830hrs, the Task Force withdrew from the coast, heading off towards the south-east. By then Rawlings had expected that the Japanese would have woken up

FAA operations: Ikishima Jima, 1 April, 1945

Easter Sunday, 1 April, 1945, was 'L-Day', the start of the amphibious assault on Okinawa. Off the Sakishima Islands V. Adm. Rawlings fully expected some form of Japanese reaction to the invasion. Flying operations began before dawn, with a reconnaissance flight over Ishigaki, the British target for the day's operations. It revealed the island's airfields were busy, suggesting they were being used as a staging post for kamikaze attacks. Their first target though, proved to be the British Task Force itself.

Key:
- Heavy AA guns
- Wireless station
- Radar station
- Seaplane base
- Barracks

EVENTS

1. 0620hrs. Reconnaissance of Ishigaki by three Hellcats (1839 NAS) reveals around 20 Japanese aircraft on Ishigaki Main airfield, and eight more at Miyara.

2. 0643hrs. First 'Ramrod' strafing attack of 20 Corsairs and Hellcats takes off but the attack is cancelled, as 15 Japanese aircraft are detected approaching from the west. Fighters are sent to reinforce the CAP over the carriers and shoot down four Zeke fighters.

3. 0645hrs – 0740hrs. TF under sustained air attack from kamikazes. All further flying operations suspended for the duration. The carrier *Indefatigable* is damaged, as is the destroyer *Ulster*.

4. 1227hrs. The only bombing strike sets off for Ishigaki 12 minutes later. At 1313hrs, it makes landfall to the south-east of Ishigaki.

5. 1310hrs. The Target Combat Air Patrol (TarCAP) of 12 Corsairs and four Hellcats approaches the island, and commences flying a CAP patrol over its centre. It remains there until the last air attack of the day is completed.

6. 1314hrs. Strike Force 'Able', of four Avengers escorted by four Corsair fighters approaches Miyara airfield and drops 16 500lb bombs over the target, putting the runway out of action.

7. 1315hrs. Strike Force 'Baker', of 12 Avengers led by Lt. Cdr. Foster (CO 849 NAS) and escorted by eight Corsairs attacks, flying 'top cover' approaches the primary target of Ishigaki Main airfield. A total of 48 5lb bombs are dropped, and again the runway is rendered unusable. Several parked aircraft are also destroyed.

8. 1320–1327hrs. After bombing their targets, the Avengers from Strikes 'Able' and 'Baker' rendezvous over Kabira Bay, before returning to their carriers. The last of the strike lands at 1410hrs.

9. 1401hrs. A 'Ramrod' sweep of 16 Corsairs takes off from the carriers at 1324hrs, and heads towards Ishigarki. After making landfall at 1400hrs, the fighters strafe Miyara and Hegina airfields, before returning to their carriers. At least three aircraft are destroyed on the ground, one at Miyara and two at Hegina.

10. One Corsair from 1834 NAS is hit by AA fire, and forced to ditch to the south of the island. Despite a search by an air sea-rescue (ASR) Walrus floatplane, the pilot is never recovered.

11. 1440hrs. The CAP screen patrolling over Ishigaki is recalled, but *en route* it carries out a 'Ramrod' attack, strafing all three Japanese airfields for a final time. By 1730hrs, the last of these fighters has landed back on the carriers.

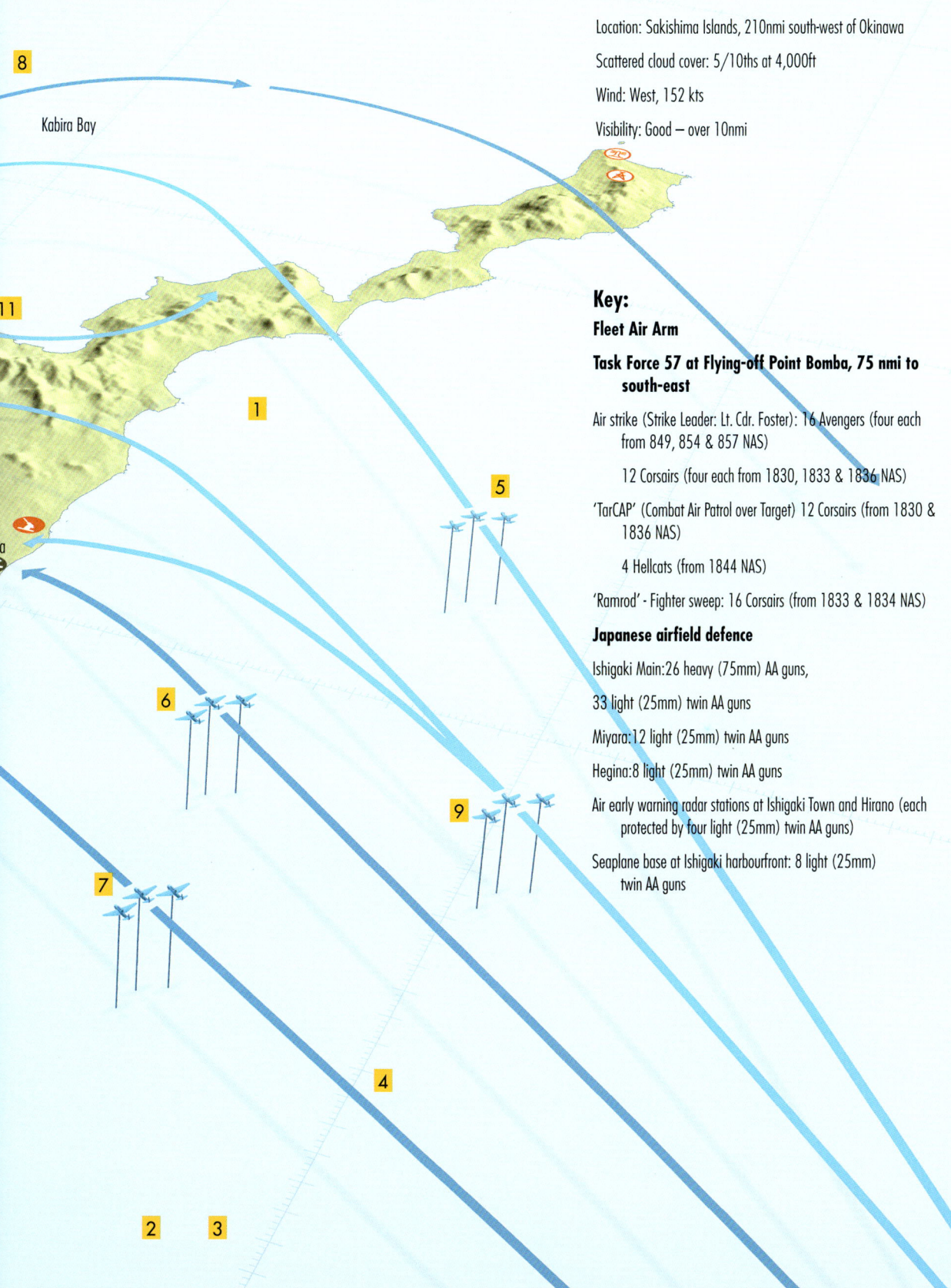

A Grumman Hellcat being ranged onto her flying-off point on the flight deck of HMS *Illustrious* in late 1944. For the Okinawa campaign, only HMS *Indomitable* had Hellcats embarked, a total of 29 fighters from 1839 and 1844 NAS.

to the threat posed by the British fleet, and so might well have attempted to send reconnaissance aircraft out to locate and shadow it during the night. They might even have attempted a nocturnal long-range air attack, although this was considered far less likely. So, aboard *Indomitable* a pair of Hellcats were kept ready throughout the night, together with two veteran pilots used for night operations. They would be launched as soon as an enemy aircraft was spotted on the radar. Unfortunately, although the Hellcats were best suited to night flying, the British versions lacked radar, and so would have to rely on the Task Force to guide them towards the shadowing aircraft. That night though, the radar screen remained blank, and the Hellcats weren't needed.

Easter Sunday morning, 1 April 1945, was 'L-Day'. That morning, the III US Marine Corps and XXIV US Army Corps landed four divisions of troops on the Hagushi beaches, on the north-western coast of Okinawa. They were supported by an immense naval bombardment and by air strikes launched from Mitscher's carriers. The initial landings went surprisingly well, and a bridgehead was established which encompassed two Japanese airfields. American casualties had been relatively light, and so the land commander, Lt Gen. Buckner, moved on to Phase II, the securing of the rest of the central part of the 65-mile-long island. This would prove a much tougher prospect, but by nightfall the Marines had sealed off the Ishikawa Isthmus, which led to the northern part of the island, while Army and USMC units had cordoned off the island's southern portion. On L-Day, the most serious opposition came from the air.

A strong CAP protected the amphibious landing fleet, but inevitably some Japanese bombers of kamikaze planes got through. At 0600hrs, as the landing ships approached the beach, a wave of kamikaze Ki-61 'Tony' aircraft appeared without warning from the north. One crashed into the port side of the crowded attack transport ship USS *Hinsdale*, damaging her engine room. The embarked troops were lucky though – only 15 were killed in the attack, and another 40 wounded. A tank landing ship was also badly damaged that morning. Then, at 1910hrs, during another air attack, a bomb struck the deck of the attack transport ship *Alpine*, killing 16 crewmen and injuring 19 more. The kamikazes also attacked American warships off the Kerama Islands, 20 miles south-west of Okinawa. There, the destroyer-minelayer USS *Adams* was damaged, and her rudders jammed. She, like the two attack transports, survived the attack, and was eventually withdrawn for repairs.

Two hundred miles to the south-west, TF 57 also had an eventful L-Day. The day began with the dawn reconnaissance of the Sakishima Islands by Hay and Luard. They noted that the main airfields on Ishigaki and Miyako had more aircraft there than usual. Presumably they were being used to stage attacks on the American fleet – or the British one. So, at 0640hrs the Ramrod fighter sweep was sent off, made up of 32 Corsairs drawn from *Illustrious* and *Victorious*. Ten minutes later, at 0650hrs, air search radars detected Japanese aircraft 75 miles to the west, approaching at 8,000ft at a speed of over 200kts. The CAP was already in place over the Task Force, but additional fighters were launched, while the Ramrod Corsairs heading for Ishigaki were diverted and vectored towards the approaching enemy planes. This would be the first test of the British fleet's defences in the campaign.

The British and Japanese aircraft clashed 40 miles to the west of the fleet. The Japanese aircraft were mainly Mitsubishi A6M Zekes (or less officially 'Zeros'), operating from airfields in northern

The battleship HMS *King George V*, flagship of V. Adm. Rawlings, operational commander of TF 57 during the Okinawa campaign. The battleship played a part in the air campaign on 4 May by shelling Hirara airfield on Miyako Jima.

Formosa, 200 miles to the west. In the first clash, four of them were shot down by Corsairs and the attacker's close formation was broken up. The individual Zeros continued to close with the British Task Force, although some were drawn into the dogfight. Others were pursued by the Corsairs, until the Japanese came within range of the Seafires which made up the British CAP. With any semblance of order lost, most of the attacking fighters didn't reach the fleet. A few though, evaded their pursuers and the CAP fighters and pressed home their attacks.

The most northerly of the four British carriers was *Indomitable*. At 0725hrs, a Zeke dived in and strafed her flight deck, killing a crewman and wounding six others as they ran for cover. The fighter then did the same to *King George V*, despite the ferocious AA fire erupting from the battleship. This time though, nobody was hurt. At the same moment, at 0728hrs, another Zeke attacked the most westerly of the carriers, *Indefatigable*. It turned out to be a kamikaze. It braved a wall of flak to crash into the base of the carrier's island on the starboard side. Fourteen of the carrier's crew were killed and many more injured. Most of these had been in the small sick bay at the base of the island, against which the fighter's 250kg bomb detonated. A fire erupted around the crashed fighter, but the flight deck's fire control teams were on the scene within seconds and began getting the blaze under control.

In the sick bay, Cdr. Chambers, the Flight Deck Officer, was chatting with the surgeon and a Seafire pilot when the kamikaze struck:

> At that moment there was the most shattering explosion, and the sick bay disintegrated in a sheet of flame. I was spun head over heels, over and over, until I got hold of a bit of jagged corner post, by which I heaved myself clear. In the steam and the din there was no sign of my two companions who had been laughing and joking a moment before. There was just a mass of dead and wounded in the area … The picture I retain of the scene is quite vivid; the

Jack mission – a Seafire pursuing a kamikaze, 1 April, 1945

At 0650hrs on the morning of 1 April a cluster of aircraft was detected on radar approaching the British Task Force from the west. At the time, TF 57 was some 80 miles south of the Sakishimas and air attacks on Ishigaki and Miyako were already under way. The Seafires tasked with forming the Combat Air Patrol (CAP) over the Task Force intercepted these Japanese aircraft 40 miles from the fleet, but a few Mitsubishi A6M Zero (or Zeke) fighters evaded the defenders and pressed on at low level, heading towards the British carriers. One of these managed to strafe *Formidable* and *King George V*, while a second crashed onto the flight deck of *Indefatigable*. Sub. Lt 'Dicky' Reynolds RNVR of 894 NAS was flying one of the CAP Seafires, and had been chasing a third Zeke as it headed towards *Indefatigable*.

Twice, Reynolds' shells hit the port wing of the Japanese fighter, but he was unable to stop it as it sped towards the carrier. At the last second the kamikaze reared up, rolled over and dived onto the carrier's flight deck. Reynolds had been concentrating on getting in another shot, and narrowly avoided crashing into the carrier himself, only turning away at the final moment. Twenty minutes later though, Reynolds had his revenge when he shot down two other Zekes before they could reach one of the British carriers. This illustration shows Reynolds' Seafire 'Merry Widow' at 0727hrs, during the final moments before the first kamikaze reached *Indefatigable*, desperately trying to get a lucky hit before the Zeke could reach the carrier. That morning, both *Formidable* and *Indefatigable* were lucky to escape serious damage, although several crewmen were killed in the attacks.

starboard wing of the Japanese plane burning on the island abaft the funnel, and a great gap from there to the flight deck, where the whole lot had blown up, leaving a hole about eight feet long in the island sick bay.

The explosion caused by the impact caused other damage too. Parts of the island were hit, including the carrier's wireless office. Three aircraft – an Avenger and two Fireflies – were damaged but deemed repairable. It could have been much worse. What saved R. Adm. Vian's flagship was its armoured flight deck. The burning wreckage was pushed over the side, and within 37 minutes the flight deck was fully operational again. If *Indomitable* had been a US carrier with a wooden flight deck, she would have been put out of action for the rest of the campaign.

The few Zekes which had penetrated that far were chased by British fighters. The kamikaze that struck *Indomitable* had been chased by a Seafire from 894 NAS, piloted by Sub. Lt 'Dicky' Reynolds, who pulled up at the last second to avoid hitting the carrier himself. Despite hitting the kamikaze, he was too late to prevent it from diving into the carrier. Reynolds was unable to stop another fighter carrying out a bomb attack on the destroyer *Ulster*, on the north-eastern side of the Task Force. It narrowly missed the weaving destroyer, but the detonation still damaged her engine room, killing one of her crew and wounding another. As the fighter pulled up from its bombing run, Reynolds swept in and shot it down. A few minutes later, Reynolds shot down another Zeke after a brief dogfight, as the last of the surviving Japanese fighters withdrew to the west.

Despite the attack on the Task Force, the day's planned air operations continued. The morning's Ramrod attack by 16 Corsairs on Hirara airfield went ahead and several planes were destroyed on the ground. This was followed by a strike on the airfield by 22 bomb-carrying Avengers. Afterwards, the airmen reported that there were significantly more Japanese aircraft using the airfield than on the previous day. In all, a total of 14 aircraft were reportedly destroyed on the ground at Hirara that morning, although some of these might well have been dummies. Meanwhile, a reconnaissance flight over Ishigaki showed the main airfield there to be quiet.

Indefatigable suffered some additional losses as the CAP fighters returned to land. This though, was due to the lumpy sea and the fragility of the Seafire rather than the kamikaze attack. Two Seafires were diverted while the mess caused by the kamikaze attack was being cleaned up. One wrecked her landing gear when touching town on *Illustrious*, while another struck the crash barrier when landing on *Victorious*, killing the pilot. Afterwards, both wrecked aircraft were ditched over the side. Ironically, only one Seafire from the CAP had been shot down – four-fifths of the day's losses to *Indefatigable*'s fighter wing had been caused by landing these fragile aircraft in lumpy seas.

During the early afternoon, small groups of enemy aircraft were detected on radar, but while some of these clashed with the Task Force CAP, none of them pressed home an attack. However, at 1730hrs, as Vian was preparing to hand tactical control back to Rawlings, two more aircraft were detected on radar, approaching from the direction of Miyako. They managed to evade the Seafires on CAP by flying into the low clouds, but they reappeared a few minutes later, two miles to the

The Supermarine Seafire was the naval version of the widely acclaimed Supermarine Spitfire. Unfortunately, while a superb land-based fighter, it lacked the robustness needed for carrier operations, largely due to its relatively fragile landing gear. This one operating with the Home Fleet simply missed the arrestor wires, but was caught by the emergency wire barrier, damaging the fighter's propeller but saving the pilot.

After Operation *Iceberg* the Sakishima Islands were bypassed by the Allies, as they concentrated on attacking the Japanese Home Islands instead. However, following the official Japanese surrender on 2 September, the islands still remained garrisoned. It was only in November that they were finally surrendered at a ceremony held on Okinawa.

east of the Task Force. This time their target was *Victorious*. Seafires dived to intercept the enemy, but found themselves fired on by the Task Force warships, and they pulled away. On the carrier *Victorious*' bridge, Capt. Denny reacted quickly, weaving his carrier to avoid the suspected kamikaze aircraft.

One hard turn by *Victorious* caused a kamikaze to almost miss the carrier completely, crashing into the edge of the flight deck's starboard side, before crashing into the sea and exploding. No real damage was caused to *Victorious*. The second one was shot down and crashed into the sea well clear of the ship. When the first 'Zeke' exploded, bits of the pilot's body were blown onto the flight deck, together with scraps of paperwork. Once translated, unsurprisingly these revealed that the British carriers were the attacker's top priority. This attack was the final one of the day. At sunset, 1856hrs, Rawlings ordered the Task Force to withdraw towards the south-east for the evening.

The day's events led to a change of plans. Originally, Rawlings had intended to withdraw to Midge that evening and to spend Monday refuelling. Now though, it was clear that the Japanese, in response to the assault on Okinawa, were using the Sakishima Islands as a staging post for kamikaze attacks, either on the British or American fleets. The ones which attacked the Americans that day had come from the Amami Islands, part of the Ryukyu archipelago which stretched up towards Kyushu, part of the Japanese homeland. However, the kamikazes which attacked TF 57 had come from Formosa, and so aircraft were probably also being moved over from the Chinese mainland, as well as from Japan. So, before refuelling, Rawlings planned to launch a large-scale Ramrod raid on the Sakishima airfields at dawn on Monday morning.

The night of 12 April was clear, with bright moonlight shining over the water. Still, there were no radar contacts during the night, and at 0510hrs on Monday 2 April, as the carriers neared their daytime flying-off point at Bango, four Hellcats were launched from *Indomitable* to conduct a reconnaissance of Ishigaki and Miyako. Two of them were piloted by Hay and Luard. However, Hay and one other pilot had to return to their carrier due to radio malfunctions. The other two pressed on though; and when the sun rose at 0606hrs, each Hellcat was circling over its assigned island. The hope had been to catch the enemy aircraft arrayed for a dawn departure. However, at both Ishigaki Main and Hirara there were no aircraft in sight.

Taking off from an aircraft carrier was a matter of wind. Before flying off or landing on, the carrier would turn into the wind, and steam at full speed. The combination greatly reduced the take-off speed needed by the aircraft to get airborne. This diagram is taken from a British wartime training manual.

At 0630hrs a Ramrod force of 17 Corsairs took off from *Victorious* and *Illustrious*, and headed towards the airfields. The Ramrod attacks on the two airfields went ahead, despite the lack of suitable targets, and two Japanese aircraft were destroyed on the ground, one on each airfield. From the wreckage, it was clear these were real aircraft rather than dummies. One of the Corsairs was damaged by ground fire over Ishigaki, and the pilot was forced to ditch close to the Task Force. He was recovered by a destroyer. During the attack, an Island CAP of Hellcats from *Indomitable* had been circling over the two islands, and one of them spotted a Zeke approaching Ishigaki from the west. After a short dogfight, the Japanese fighter was shot down. By 1045hrs, all of the aircraft had been recovered, and Vian handed over tactical control of the Task Force to Rawlings. He gave the order that had the whole fleet turn away towards the south-east and begin the 280-mile voyage to Rendezvous Area Midge, where the Fleet Train's tankers and escort carriers were waiting for them.

Adms Nimitz and Spruance were keen to maintain the pressure on the Sakishima airfields while TF 57 was away refuelling. So, TG 58.1, Mitscher's US Fast Carrier Force of three fleet carriers (*Bennington*, *Hornet* and *Wasp*) and two light carriers (USS *Belleau Wood* and USS *San Jacinto*), moved down from its position west of Okinawa to fill the void. Throughout Tuesday, Wednesday and Thursday, the core of the US Fifth Fleet's carriers would be away from Okinawa, and so leave the forces there stripped of much of their air cover. This was a gamble, but the weather conditions in the Philippine Sea meant this temporary relocation would be a more lengthy one than Spruance or Mitscher had anticipated.

In this view of the centre of Hirara airfield, taken from the strike leader's aircraft during one of the regular bombing attacks on the field, the dust and debris thrown up by the bomb detonations is lightened by coral dust.

It took the best part of 18 hours for TF 57 to steam to the rendezvous, but Midge was reached at dawn on Tuesday 3 April. The rendezvous area was extensive, covering a few 100 miles of sea, and it took a few hours to locate the tankers. By then, the seas had become too rough to carry out the refuelling, and the 20kt fresh breeze didn't help. So, Rawlings ordered both the Task Force and the Fleet Train detachment to steam west to Rendezvous Area Mosquito, 250 miles away, in the hope of finding better conditions there. They arrived there at dawn on Wednesday, and conditions were indeed a little better – at least good enough to attempt the refuelling. The RAS began at 0730hrs, but due to the conditions it all took much longer than anticipated. Several fuel hoses parted, and couplings broke, and the Fleet Train still lacked the spares it needed to replace them.

However, the escort carrier *Slinger* managed to fly off 22 replacement aircraft, which landed successfully on the relevant carriers – a mixture of Seafires, Corsairs, Avengers and Fireflies. Two unserviceable aircraft from *Indefatigable* were also shipped across amid rough seas and winched aboard *Slinger*. Rather than being transported back to Sydney, the Fleet Area Maintenance Group had established itself in Leyte in the Philippines, just over 600 miles away to the south. Once repaired, the aircraft would be embarked in *Speaker*, and would return to their parent squadrons. While the air transfer was relatively speedy, the refuelling was all taking much longer than Rawlings wanted. He felt it was imperative that the Task Force be back in position off the Sakishima Islands by dawn the following day.

So, at noon he ordered the larger ships still waiting for fuel to limit their intake to just over 50 per cent of their capacity. Then, at 1730hrs, he ordered the tankers to stop refuelling. This left his fleet 12 hours to cover the 220 miles to their dawn flying-off point. So, the British warships set off towards the north-east at 20kts, with many of them, including the fleet flagship, with her fuel tanks half empty. The carriers had been refuelled first, and so were fully topped up. However, they only had enough aviation fuel aboard for two days of flying operations. Having spoken to Vian though, who in turn had discussed the fuel situation with his leading subordinates, Rawlings thought it was enough. Far more important was the Task Force's return to its station, allowing Mitscher's carriers to return to Okinawa, where the threat of a Japanese attack was much greater.

The kamikazes strike

Sure enough, the American carriers moved off to the east that night, as the British ones moved up to take their place. By dawn on Friday 6 April, Rawlings' Task Force was in place at Flying-off Point Bango, south of Miyako, and aboard the carriers the aircraft were ranged on deck, ready for the first strike of the day. Approximately 160 miles to the north-west,

The preferred method of conducting kamikaze attacks was noted in this US Naval pamphlet, which was circulated to TF 57 before it reached the Sakishima Islands. A kamikaze aircraft would dive at an angle of 30–40°, at maximum speed, from a height of more than 12,000ft. The speed of the dive reduced the risk of the aircraft being shot down during its final approach.

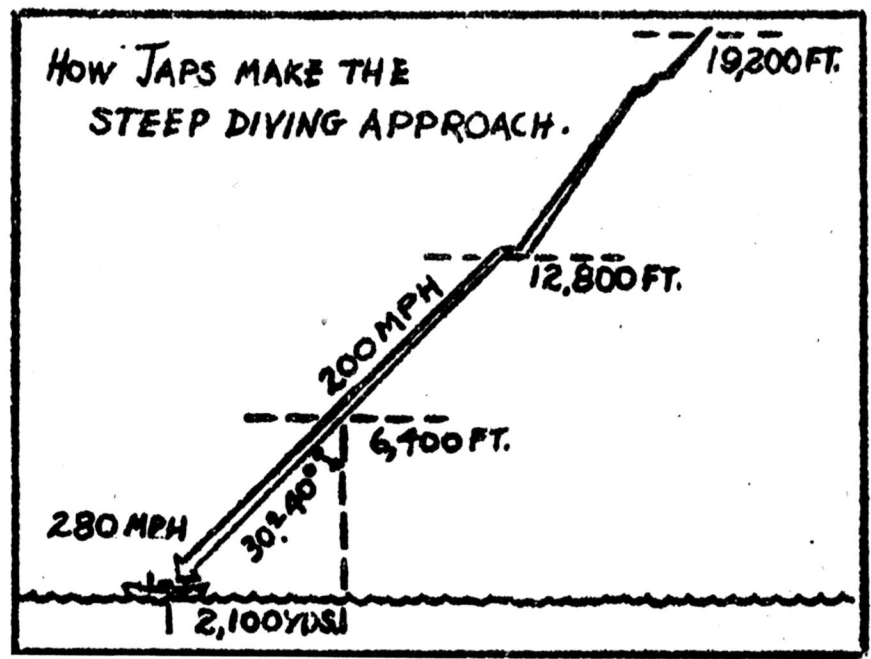

Mitscher's US Fast Carrier Force was also in position off Okinawa to deal with whatever the day might bring. It was just as well. While on Okinawa the initial assault had gone well, the Marines were making slow progress advancing up the narrow northern portion of the island. In the south though, the American advance had halted in front of the 'Shuri Barrier', a line of strong defensive positions which spanned the island from east to west. From that point on, the going would become much tougher – and much bloodier.

So, Lt Gen. Buckner would need all the naval strike aircraft he could get to pound these Japanese defences. However, intelligence reports from intercepted radio traffic suggested that the Japanese were planning a major operation against the US Fifth Fleet. Until then, Japanese air activity had been sporadic over Okinawa, as the Japanese had needed time to marshal their assets. Now, they had the means to launch a series of large and sustained kamikaze attacks against Spruance's ships, using bases further up the chain of the Ryukyu Islands which stretched from Okinawa to the Japanese homeland. These massed kamikaze attacks were codenamed 'Kikusui', and their ferocity would take Spruance and Mitscher by surprise. The British would also not be spared from the Kikusui wave.

TF 57 resumed operations on 6 April by flying off another four Hellcats before dawn. They encountered heavy cloud over the islands, but they saw eight enemy aircraft in the twilight on Ishigaki and strafed them. No airborne activity was seen, and the fleet and Target CAPS were launched at 0630hrs to dominate the skies over the Sakishima Islands. The fighters reported that the runways on Miyako had all been repaired and were operational, so a strike was launched in the afternoon to crater them. A second strike was frustrated by low cloud, but it managed to bomb targets of opportunity through gaps. A shadow was detected on radar, but it evaded pursuit into the cloud and escaped.

At 1655hrs, the fighter direction frequencies were jammed, causing some disorganization, and bogeys were detected on radar 50 miles to the north. Four enemy aircraft broke out of the cloud at 1700hrs in steep dives and one aimed at *Illustrious*, which took radical evasive action, turning with full helm. The kamikaze failed to match the turn, but its wing tip hit the island and carried away a radar aerial before it crashed into the water, its bomb exploding on impact. The blast damaged two Corsairs in the deck park. Three other Japanese aircraft

As well as damaging the flight deck, the resulting fire from the kamikaze attack on HMS *Formidable* on 4 May destroyed 11 aircraft. However, the blaze was quickly extinguished and the debris was pushed over the side, clearing the way for the resumption of flight deck operations – something which would have been nigh-on impossible in a wooden-decked US carrier.

were shot down by the CAP, another was shot down by a destroyer, while one of the aircraft strafed on the ground was deemed to have been destroyed. British aircraft losses for the day were four, one of which was a Seafire shot down by the fleet's own gunfire, with the loss of the pilots. The other three were due to mechanical problems. As usual, TF 57 disengaged to the south-east after dusk.

Adm. Rawlings had intended to close the coast of Ishigaki and have his two battleships bombard the airfields to save aircraft fuel on the next day, but after receiving a signal from CINC PAC warning of an all-out enemy air attack on the Allied fleets on Saturday 7 April, he decided to keep TF 57 concentrated in one place and continued to use air strikes and Target CAPs over the islands. Between 0610hrs and dusk, three strikes were flown to crater all the enemy runways and leave them unserviceable. It was a little disappointing that each morning the runways had been patched up. Much of this lay in the Royal Navy's ordnance – big bombs, which were designed for attacking well-protected warships such as *Tirpitz*, rather than thinly paved runways or grass airstrips. It seems that the small, neat holes they left were fairly easy to repair.

The bomb craters in the paved runways of Ishigaki Main had been filled in, as had those at Hirara and Nobara. Hegina and Miyara on Ishigaki and Sukuma on Miyako remained cratered, probably because the Japanese lacked the manpower to repair all of them. Still, Vian took some comfort from the report that by Saturday afternoon, all six of the island's airfields were out of action. This made it less likely that the Japanese could use these airstrips as staging posts for kamikaze attacks. The other method of deterring further kamikaze strikes was to maintain the strong Target CAP of fighters over the enemy airfields throughout the hours of daylight. All of the Corsairs and Hellcats used for this were urged to strafe any targets of opportunity they came across, while some of the Hellcats also carried 500lb bombs, for the same purpose. By sunset on Saturday, as the fleet withdrew for the night, Vian and Rawlings, while frustrated, felt they had at least fulfilled their mission – until the bombing had to be repeated all over again.

First though, TF 57 needed to refuel. This time, the British Fleet Train was waiting in a predominantly American refuelling location, Cootie One. It had the advantage of being closer – just 160 miles south of Bango and 200 miles south-east of Bomba. On schedule, the four tankers (*Arndale*, *Dingledale*, *San Amado* and *Aese Mersk*) were sighted, in company with their escort, as well as the escort carriers HMS *Speaker* and HMS *Ruler*. There, while the refuelling continued in largely favourable sea conditions, Rawlings was joined by some

The final death dive of a kamikaze – a Zeke fighter. While many of these attacked using a steep dive, aiming for the stern of the carriers, some opted for a shallower approach, to present less of a target to the fleet's AA guns. This one, which overshot its target, carried a 250kg bomb to increase the effectiveness of the strike.

reinforcements – the Fiji-class light cruiser HMCS *Uganda*, and the U/V class destroyers HMS *Urchin* and HMS *Ursa*. These were particularly welcome, as during the previous week the W-class destroyer HMS *Whelp* had developed defects. She then, was detached from the Task Force, and sent off to Leyte in the Philippines for repairs.

Vian also took the opportunity to fly over from *Indomitable* to inspect the damage on *Indefatigable* and *Illustrious*. On board them, Capt. Graham and Capt. Stephens assured the admiral that they were still fully operational. The wounded were also transferred to *Ruler*, to be forwarded on from Leyte to Sydney, and replacement aircraft and aircrews were flown over from the two escort carriers. The refuelling was completed successfully in the late afternoon of Monday 9 April. The refuelling, while arduous for the fleet's seamen, gave the air crews, maintenance staff and flight deck crews a chance to rest after what had been a stressful period of nearly continuous flying operations.

Rawlings had intended to return to Flying-off Point Bango, and for the next two days, 10–11 April, carry out a repeat of previous attacks: the now somewhat boring and repetitive cratering of the Sakishima airfields, and the flying of Target CAP missions over the islands.

Kamikaze pilots from the Imperial Japanese Navy preparing to carry out an attack, in 1945. A number of rituals, prayers and speeches preceded these one-way missions. While kamikaze attacks sacrificed Japan's dwindling supply of pilots, aircraft and fuel, they were deemed effective enough to make this an acceptable degree of loss in order to safeguard the Japanese homeland.

After that, TF 57 would head south to Leyte, for a short period of 'replenishment and rehabilitation'. Defects in the ships would be repaired, they would be replenished and stored, and the crew would be granted local leave. The fleshpots of Leyte were an attractive prospect for many of the men of TF 57. However, an intelligence report and a request from Adm. Spruance changed all that. Since 'L-Day' on 1 April, the Fifth Fleet had come under repeated kamikaze attacks. The carrier USS *Hancock* had been damaged, as had the battleship *Maryland* and the escort carrier *Wake Island*. 13 destroyers had also been damaged, and three more sunk or scuttled.

Spruance said that while the majority of the kamikaze attacks had come from Kyushu in the Japanese homeland, a number – the most effective – had attacked the fleet from bases in Formosa. While TF 57 had done a good job of denying the enemy the Sakishima airfields as staging posts, Japanese bombers and fighters equipped with long-range fuel tanks had proved that they could reach Okinawa from airfields in northern Formosa. As this flight path of a little over 300 miles had been routed to the north of the Sakishima chain, the British had been unaware of these attacks. Spruance's request was that Rawlings leave the attacks on the Sakishima airfields for a few days, and instead, concentrate on the Formosan airfields. This time TF 57 wouldn't be on its own. Aircraft from Gen. MacArthur's South-West Pacific Area would support the British, flying from bases in the Philippines.

Operation *Iceberg Oolong*

This Formosa problem had been known by Admiral Spruance as early as Sunday 8 April. His solution, apart from redeploying his fleet to be better prepared for attacks from the south-west, was to ask Adm. Nimitz for permission to redeploy TF 57 to try and deal with the problem. Nimitz sent through his approval of the scheme on Monday morning, while the British fleet was still refuelling at Cootie. In the absence of TF 57, the CAP over the Sakishima chain was being maintained by American escort carriers: Unit One of the Support Carrier Group, which was part of R. Adm. Blandy's Task Group 52. Unit One's commander, R. Adm. Sprague, confirmed that his seven escort carriers could cover the Sakishimas for a few more days. So, Spruance was able to contact Rawlings, and request his help.

As expected, Rawlings agreed immediately. The intention was to carry out a series of strikes against the two main airfields in northern Formosa, Shinchiku and Matsuyama.

Japanese kamikaze pilots undertaking a pre-attack briefing. Although no kamikaze pilots returned to share their experience, enough had been gleaned from supporting Japanese aircraft to determine that attacking carriers from astern offered the greatest range of options during the final moments of the attack.

The Shinchiku airfield was sited near the north-western coast of the island, beside the port city of the same name (now Hsinchu). Matsuyama airfield was 40 miles to the north-east, to the north of the city of Taipei. The site, now the Taipei Songshan Airport, lay beside the Chi-Lung Ho River amid tea plantations. A line of mountains, which ran down the spine of Formosa, lay between the two Japanese airfields and the planned flying-off point, 65 miles off the coast in the Philippine Sea, to the south-east of Taipei. As Vian and his staff began planning for this new operation, Spruance assured Rawlings that Gen. MacArthur's South-West Pacific Command (SWPA) would order the US Fifth Air Force based in the Philippines to distract the Japanese, by bombing airfields in southern Formosa.

In fact, Maj. Gen. Kenney's Fifth Air Force only performed a fraction of the attacks Nimitz had requested. Gen. MacArthur, it seems, had other priorities. Of the 25,000 bombing and escort sorties requested, using B-24 Liberators and B-25 Mitchells, escorted by P-47 Thunderbolts and P-51 Mustangs, less than a tenth were carried out that April, just 1,636, representing four bombing missions, each composed of two medium and two heavy Bombardment Groups and their fighter escorts. Still, with over 280 bombers in each of these missions, each targeting an airfield in south-west Formosa, on paper these attacks still dwarfed anything TF 57 could achieve. In practice though, not only were the bombing missions poorly directed and lacked precision, but the Japanese had also moved their aircraft north, so little real damage was done.

For TF 57, this operation, codenamed *Iceberg Oolong*, would involve every Avenger at its disposal. The plan conceived by Vian was to begin on 11 April with a dawn strike on Matsuyama, from a flying-off point 95 miles to the south-east. Once the aircraft were recovered the Task Force would retire during the night, then return to the same flying-off point, to launch another dawn attack, this time on Shinchiku, at dawn on 12 April. After the aircraft returned, the Task Force would withdraw to refuel. Each strike would involve all the available Avengers, supported by a substantial escort of Corsairs and Hellcats. Other fighters would precede the main strike with a Ramrod mission, strafing the airfields 20 minutes before the bombers arrived. In addition, 20 Seafires from *Indefatigable* would be airborne at any one time, providing a CAP cover for the Task Force.

The airmen serving in the BPF were very young – the majority were in their early twenties. Sub. Lt Ralph Jameson RNVR, aged 23, seen here in the cockpit of his Fairey Firefly, was typical of these Fleet Air Arm servicemen.

As TF 57 was operating just 50 miles off the coast of Formosa, there was a substantial likelihood that the fleet would be attacked. So, as well as a stronger CAP than usual, 20 rather than 16 Seafires in the air at any one time, other fighters were held ready on the other three carriers to augment the Seafires if required. For this operation, the CAP was split into four groups, each operating at a set altitude between 3,000 and 20,000ft. In previous attacks, the Japanese kamikazes had appeared at a variety of heights, from 25,000ft down to sea level. This way the Seafires would be ready for them. The other important provision was for ASR support. As before, the USS *Kingfisher* was moved to a position off the north-eastern coast of Formosa, along the line of the air strike on Matsuyama. Other American submarines would be sent to the area too, while TF 52 would send US Navy ASR aircraft, to patrol the area between the flying-off point and the Formosan coast.

However, dawn on Wednesday 11 April revealed low cloud over Formosa, at around 1,000ft, and persistent rain. So, Vian decided to postpone the operation for 24 hours. US Navy meteorologists predicted an improvement in conditions before dawn the following day. Sure enough, the weather improved during the night, and dawn on Thursday 12 April revealed

Corsairs returning to their carriers after a Ramrod mission over Ishigaki Jima. Essentially, the Ramrod was a fighter sweep over one or more airfields, which strafed any aircraft on the runways or in the dispersal bays, and shot up any other targets of opportunity that it found.

favourable flying conditions. So, Operation *Iceberg Oolong* would go ahead. This time though, the plan had been altered. Both Japanese airfields would be attacked at the same time, to reduce the risk of the enemy moving aircraft to other airfields in between the strikes.

At 0600hrs on Thursday 12 April, the 20 Seafires that made up the initial CAP force were flown off and took up their positions over the Task Force. The force had been reduced by a four-fighter flight, and these were kept ranged on deck to be launched if an enemy attack was detected. Sure enough, as the main strikes were being ranged on deck, four enemy aircraft were detected, which turned out to be three Zekes and a Kawasaki Ki-61 Tony, flying eastwards from Formosa to the north of the Task Force. Two flights of Seafires from *Indefatigable*'s 887 NAS intercepted them, and in the dogfight that followed one of the enemy Zekes was shot down by Sub. Lt Kernaghan of 894 NAS, before the rest disappeared into the clouds and headed back towards Formosa.

At 0715hrs, the two strikes took off, one bound for each of the two target airfields. Each strike was made up of 24 Avengers and 20 fighters, a mixture of Corsairs and Hellcats. The planned initial Ramrod attack had been adapted, so instead half the fighter escort would carry out the Ramrod attack, while the others remained close to the bombers. The strikes headed off towards the north-west, but on reaching the coast they found the Formosan highlands

Japanese kamikazes, Yonakuni Island, 12 April, 1945

Due to a build-up of Japanese kamikaze aircraft on Formosa, on 10 April, Adm. Spruance requested that for two days TF 57 attack airfields there, rather than ones in the Sakishimas. Rain delayed the start of this, but the air attacks finally began at dawn on 12 April, with the British carriers operating from a new flying-off point 100 miles to the east of Formosa. While these strikes were being carried out, a US Navy air-sea-rescue (ASR) float plane was stationed 30 miles to the north of the British Task Force, in case any damaged British aircraft had to ditch in the sea there as they headed home. Their patrol area was near Yonakuni Island, midway between Formosa and Iriomote Jima in the Sakishima chain. Two Fairy Fireflies of 1770 NAS were launched from HMS *Indefatigable* to protect the ASR aircraft, and at 1355hrs they began their patrol over the island.

Some 25 minutes later, five Japanese fighters were detected on radar heading towards them from the east. The Fireflies intercepted them, and they turned out to be Ki-51 Sonia dive-bombers, equipped as kamikazes. It seems these were heading east to attack the US Fleet off Okinawa. The two Fireflies managed to approach them without being seen, and both aircraft shot down a Sonia in their first pass. Within a few minutes three of the dive bombers had been shot down, while the fourth was damaged. However, it managed to crash-land on Yonakuni. It was a fairly easy victory – the Sonias were laden with 250kg bombs, heavier than their normal payload – for this one-way mission. They also lacked a rear-gunner, which made them easy prey for the two Fireflies.

were covered in thick cloud. So, they followed the coast towards the north and hugged it, keeping just out to sea. After passing the headlands of Yang-liao Pi and Pi-t'ou Chiao, they banked inland near to the port city of Chi-Lung Chiang (now Keelung), following the main road from there until they reached Taipei. There the two strikes separated, with one forming up to attack Matsuyama and the other heading for Shinchiku.

Shinchiku airfield was successfully located and bombed by the Avengers of 820 and 857 NAS, while the Ramrod fighters strafed the area. Several enemy aircraft were spotted there in dispersal bays. Enemy ground fire was found to be intense and accurate. However, Matsuyama airfield was wreathed in low-lying cloud, lying at around 2,000ft. Reluctantly, Lt Col. Hay, who led the strike, switched to the strike's alternative target, the port of Keelung itself. There, the Avengers of 849 and 854 NAS bombed the docks, ships in the harbour and even a nearby chemical plant. One of the Avengers didn't return, presumably having crashed over the island. Spectacular though this strike was, it didn't help reduce the threat posed by kamikazes operating from Matsuyama. So, as there were no enemy aircraft in the area, Hay detached the two Ramrod flights, and as the Avengers headed for home, he headed towards Matsuyama, and dropped down low beneath the cloud.

They found the airfield, and leading the attack in his Hellcat, Hay and those behind him strafed the runway, disposal bays and fuel dumps. Once again, there was little in the way of AA fire. During the attack, Hay counted 12 enemy aircraft on the ground, and he managed to destroy one during his strafing attack. There was no sign of any CAP over the airfields either, and so the Ramrod fighters climbed away, and headed after the rest of the strike, which was then on its way back to the carriers. Despite checking all around, the groups of strike aircraft returned unmolested – no Japanese aircraft attempted to attack them during their return flight. However, a damaged Corsair of 1833 NAS embarked on *Illustrious* had to ditch, and the pilot was never recovered. After both bombing attacks, enjoying the lack of enemy air activity, the escorts strafed targets of opportunity before they left the island, including railways and bridges.

The only clash that morning took place 30 miles to the north of the Task Force, where a US Navy Martin PBI Mariner float plane patrolled over Yonakuni Island, the westernmost of the Sakishima chain. It was there to provide ASR cover for the British strikes. The Task Force sent two Fireflies from *Indefatigable*'s 1770 NAS to provide CAP cover for it, and it was these British fighter-bombers which spotted a flight of five Mitsubishi Ki-51 'Sonia' dive bombers pass to the north of the small island. Presumably they were on their way from Formosa to Okinawa. They managed to attack the dive bombers without being seen, and each Firefly shot down two of them. The fifth dive bomber was damaged, but managed to escape.

Another American-built fighter, the Grumman Hellcat was essentially a larger and more powerful version of the Grumman Wildcat, which the Fleet Air Arm called the Martlet. These were extremely manoeuvrable and responsive aircraft and were well liked by their pilots. This one is pictured ranged for take-off from HMS *Indomitable*.

There were other clashes that day too. Another Sonia, possibly the damaged one, landed on an emergency strip on Yonakuni after developing an engine problem. It was spotted by one of the patrolling Mariners, and a Fleet Air Arm Corsair returning to the Task Force dived down and strafed it, destroying the aircraft before climbing away to rejoin his companions. Meanwhile, having returned to their carrier, the Hellcats and Corsairs of *Indomitable*, *Victorious* and *Illustrious* were refuelled, and took over CAP duties from the Seafires. At 1530hrs, a Hellcat of 1839 NAS surprised and shot down a lone Zeke to the north-west of the Task Force, close to the Formosan shore. The only serious threat to the Task Force that day though, came from a group of eight bogeys, detected on American SM-1 air warning radar that had been fitted in *Indefatigable*, as they approached the British fleet from the direction of Ishigaki.

A flight of three Hellcats from the CAP were vectored to intercept them, 30 miles to the north-east of the Task Force. Another two flights of Corsairs took off from *Illustrious* and *Victorious* too to support them. In a ten-minute dogfight, the three Hellcats shot down four Nakajima Ki-43 Oscar fighters and a Ki-61 Tony. In return, one of the Hellcats was badly damaged, but it managed to limp back to *Indomitable*. Then, when the Corsairs arrived, Lt Cdr Edmunson shot down a Zeke. The remaining Japanese fighters evaded their pursuers and returned to Ishigaki. That ended the day's flying, and the tally sheet showed 16 Japanese aircraft destroyed by the Fleet Air Arm for the loss of three British aircraft. However, the strikes hadn't done much to reduce the kamikaze threat.

That Thursday (12 April), the kamikazes had pummelled US Fifth Fleet. Intelligence reports suggested a major attack was coming, and Spruance adopted a defensive formation. All afternoon, from 1300hrs on, groups of a dozen or so aircraft attacked the fleet, starting with the destroyers on radar picket. The Americans had sent up a large CAP force, and over 80 Japanese aircraft were shot down in the skies over Amami and Kikai, 150 miles from the American fleet, away to the north-east up the Ryukyu chain. It wasn't enough, and groups penetrated this tripwire CAP screen, to reach the fleet itself. Another CAP screen of 72 fighters protected the American carriers. Even so, too many of the attackers got through. Worse, the Japanese used nine rocket-propelled one-man suicide bombs, one of which sank the destroyer USS *Mannert L. Abele*, and damaged two more. In all, 163 aircraft took part in these attacks over two days, about 49 of which were kamikaze attacks.

By the end of the day, the battleship USS *Tennessee* had been damaged when a kamikaze hit her bridge, while one destroyer had been sunk and six more damaged. Two tank landing ships had been damaged and another sunk. Fortunately for Spruance, his precious carriers had been spared. So, he requested that Rawlings do what he could to help ease the pressure. As Rawlings put it, even if the Formosa and Sakishima operations didn't stem the attacks, at least the British could provide an additional target for the Japanese kamikazes, which might 'take some of the weight'. So TF 57 would remain on station for a few more days, until the situation improved. Dawn then, on Friday found the Task Force back on its flying-off point to the east of Formosa.

The day began with a surprise pre-dawn attack at 0545hrs by four Japanese dive bombers, which approached the Task Force from the north. Four Hellcats were scrambled from *Indomitable*, but they weren't in position before the Japanese dive bombed the carrier. All their four 250kg bombs missed though, and one of the dive-bombers, now identified as Japanese Navy Aicha D3A 'Vals', was shot down. Unfortunately, so was one of the Hellcats, which came in too close and was downed by its own carrier's AA guns. The Japanese survivors then flew off, chased by the Hellcats. At 0610hrs, four more bogeys were detected on radar, and four Corsairs of 1830 NAS were launched and sent to intercept them. The clash took place 20 miles north of the fleet, and ended with two Zekes shot down and the other two driven off.

At 0645hrs the two daily air strikes were launched and, after forming up the Avengers and their escorts, headed off towards the north-west and the Formosan coast. Once again, the targets were Shinchiku and Matsuyama. The Royal Marine pilot Lt Col. Hay of *Victorious* 849 NAS led the Matsuyama attack, and afterwards he described what had happened:

> We took off to strike Matsuyama airfield, Formosa, at 06.45 and departed at 07.05 – surely a record! A landfall was made at 07.30 with visibility of 30 miles and 10/10ths cloud at 6,000ft. Cloud deteriorated over the hills, so I ordered the strike to proceed round the coast. This they did, climbing to 8,000ft. Unfortunately, a solid layer of cloud built up right over the airfield and prevented a detailed examination of the target. The cloud layer was 1,000ft thick with a base of 3,000ft. I informed strike leader D.R. Foster and orbited overhead looking for a gap. He eventually decided to bomb after diving through cloud.

Watching the action unfold from a low altitude, Hay continued: 'From down below I observed many bombs striking the airfield until it was covered in brown smoke and dust. There was no flak before the bombing, but the moment the bombers appeared below 3,000ft, every gun went into action. They were obviously waiting.' Still, the attacking Avengers dropped their bombs with commendable accuracy, and made it safely away. However, six of the bombers hadn't managed to join in the attack, and so tried to find targets of opportunity as the strike headed back towards the coast. Again, Hay picked up the narrative, 'On withdrawal one Avenger bombed a factory. I caught a passenger train which was skulking in a tunnel, but rather carelessly had left the engine sticking out. We then shot up a few junks, and went on to Giran where approximately twelve aircraft of various types were spotted.'

Giran was another paved airfield, albeit a smaller one, south of Yilan City. There, the British airmen strafed a twin-engined plane on the ground, possibly a Dinah reconnaissance aircraft, but were disappointed when it failed to explode in a fireball. It was probably a dummy. The strike then returned to the carriers. Afterwards Hay concluded, that; 'Considering the weather, I think the strike was a fine piece of work.' The attack on Shinchiku was also successful. With the airfield bombed heavily and several aircraft and buildings strafed. This time, AA fire was less effective than before and the aircraft all made it away without being hit. They too then returned to the fleet. What was noticeable though, was the lack of any CAP over the island. In fact, apart from the ones probing the defences of the fleet, no enemy aircraft were seen in the air that day.

At 1900hrs, half an hour after sunset, the Task Force withdrew to the east, to a pre-arranged rendezvous at Rendezvous Area Cootie. As they steamed away from Formosa, radio reports reached them that the US President Franklin D. Roosevelt had died the previous day. This cast a somewhat sombre tone over what was otherwise an evening of celebration for a job well done. Before the plea for help from Adm. Spruance, TF 57 had been scheduled to head south to Leyte after being refuelled. Now though, given the threat to the US Fifth Fleet, Rawlings offered to carry out another two days of operations over the Sakishima Islands. Spruance readily accepted the offer, as it allowed him to recall R. Adm. Sprague's seven escort carriers stationed there.

At dawn on Saturday 14 April, TF 57 arrived at Rendezvous Area Cootie, located the waiting tankers and began refuelling.

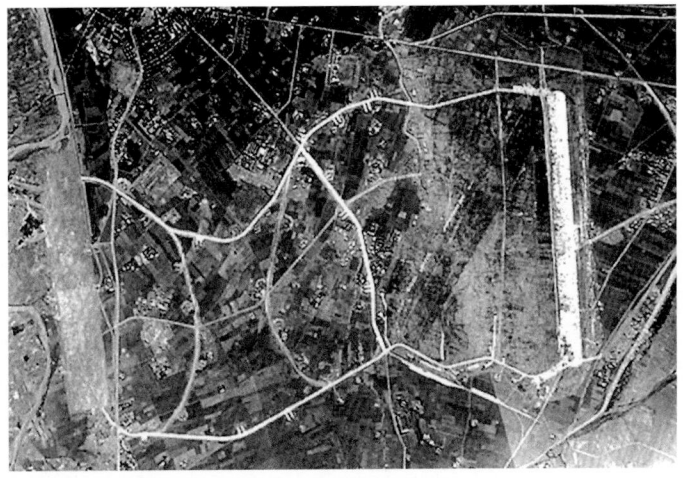

The single paved airstrip at Giran airfield in north-eastern Formosa (now Taiwan), which was attacked by aircraft from TF 59 on 13 April, during Operation *Iceberg Oolong*. It was a known 'feeder airfield' for bombers and kamikaze aircraft, which would then use the Sakishimas as a staging post for attacks on the US Fifth Fleet.

Just as importantly, the carrier *Formidable* was there too, ready to join the fleet. Rawlings and Vian decided to send *Illustrious* to Leyte for repairs, which was suffering from 'old wounds', defects resulting from damage earlier in the war. She was escorted by the destroyers *Urania* and *Quality*. This meant that the strength of the carrier strike force remained at four fleet carriers. Still, the escort carriers accompanying the tankers also brought replacement pilots, which meant that the Task Force was almost back up to strength for its next visit to the Sakishimas. The refuelling was completed on Sunday afternoon, so Rawlings set a course back towards the island chain and its airfields.

Return to the Sakishimas

The loss of *Illustrious* didn't alter the number of Corsairs available, as this matched the quantity embarked in *Formidable*. The reinforcing carrier also carried three more Avengers than *Illustrious*. Still, owing to the general shortage of fighter aircraft on the carriers, due largely to non-operational damage to the Seafires embarked in *Indefatigable*, no radar picket cruisers and destroyers were stationed on Monday 16 April. The first strike of the day took off shortly after dawn at 0630hrs, made up of 16 Avengers and 12 escorting fighters. Its objective was to bomb the Ishigaki airfields. A second strike of the same size was launched at 1230hrs to finish the job of bombing the island's three airfields. The result was that by early afternoon, all of the runways on Ishigaki had been put out of action. A Target CAP of 12 Corsairs was also positioned over the island for the duration of the two strikes.

At Miyako, the pre-strike reconnaissance had revealed that a lot of effort had been made by the Japanese to repair the airfields there after the departure of the American carriers which had been filling in for the British during Operation *Iceberg Oolong*. All three airfields there were found to be operational. However, that didn't last long. Two air strikes were launched against the Miyako airfields during the day, of similar size to the ones against Ishigaki. Again, a Target CAP of 12 Corsairs was also sent to ensure control of the skies

Air strike on Hirara airfield, Miyako Jima, 17 April, 1945

By 17 April, TF 57 had been operating off the Sakishima Islands for almost a month, and so the carrier air crews were fully aware of what was facing them. That day, a new system was used for Fleet Air Arm air operations over the archipelago's Japanese airfields. First, a high-level CAP force of Corsairs and/or Hellcats was sent up over the target island shortly before dawn. The job of this 'TarCAP' was to intercept any enemy aircraft trying to reinforce these airfields or gathering for an attack on either the British or American fleets. A second CAP was sent up to protect the British Task Force itself. The TarCAP inspected the Japanese airfields, and only then was the day's strike planned. For instance, on 17 April this revealed that the runways on Ishigaki Jima were still unserviceable after previous attacks, so all the strikes were sent to Miyako Jima instead.

While the TarCAP fought isolated Japanese fighters overhead, shooting down three Zekes for no British loss, three waves of Avengers struck the three airfields on Miyako Jima. The largest of these airfields was Hirara airfield, which had three runways that crossed each other in the centre of the airfield. That forenoon the attack on Hirara was carried out by 16 Avengers from 849 NAS (HMS *Victorious*) and 857 NAS (HMS *Indomitable*). These dive bombers approached from different directions to throw off fire from the well-defended airfield. However, they all concentrated on the area where the three runways intersected. In all, 64 bombs were dropped, cratering all the runways, and leaving them unserviceable. This illustration shows an Avenger releasing its bombs, while further ahead another has just pulled out of its dive. While the attack was proceeding, accompanying Corsairs strafed the airfield's anti-aircraft positions, to supress Japanese fire. In the end, only one Avenger was damaged in the attack, but the three crewmen were rescued. The attack left the packed-coral runways badly cratered, but in the night Japanese engineers would do their best to repair them before the whole operation was repeated. Only by regular attacks could TF 57 prevent the Japanese from using these airfields to launch attacks on the British or American task forces.

over the island. By mid-afternoon it was clear that all of the island's runways had been cratered so extensively that they were unserviceable. All in all, it was a productive day for the Task Force. Although there wasn't any enemy air activity that day, in the afternoon two bogeys were detected on air warning radar, approaching the fleet at high speed from the west. These then vanished from the screen. It was felt likely that these were rocket-powered human bombs, of the kind deployed against the Fifth Fleet. These though, seemed to have misjudged the range to Flying-off Point Bango, and the bombs crashed into the sea well to the west of the Task Force.

After withdrawing for the night, TF 57 was back on station before dawn on Tuesday morning, 17 April. This time Ishigaki was dropped as a target, as a pre-dawn reconnaissance had revealed that no attempt had been made to repair any of the airfields there. Work had been done at Miyako though, and so it became the sole target for the day's strikes. Throughout the day, three strikes were launched against the three Miyako airfields. By the end of the second strike, the runways at Hirara, Sukuma and Nobara were deemed out of action. The third strike had already been prepared, so it was sent ahead, but this time its targets were the island's headquarters buildings, barracks and other military targets. The aim was to downgrade the Japanese garrison's ability to coordinate the repair of the runways. Before darkness fell, the Task Force had withdrawn.

The intention was to head for Leyte, but once again Rawlings offered Spruance his support in adding a third day of air strikes against the Sakishimas, to better prevent the use of the airfields there as staging posts for kamikaze attacks. Spruance accepted the offer, and so, after the fleet refuelled at Rendezvous Area Mosquito, 240 miles from Bango, the British warships headed back to the islands. The replenishment lasted two days, as Vian insisted on a break from normal flying routine so that his carrier crews could carry out vital maintenance work on their aircraft. During all this, the Hellcats from the escort carriers of the Fleet Train provided a CAP screen overhead. In addition, the loss of the two destroyers, HMS *Urania* and HMS *Quality* detached to escort *Illustrious* was made up by reinforcements, the destroyers *Napier*, *Norman* and *Nepal*, under the charge of Capt. Buchanan of *Napier*, commander of the 7th Destroyer Flotilla.

The Task Force headed north during the night, and by dawn on Friday 20 April it had reached its flying-off point. For this operation though, the last before the fleet's visit to Leyte, Vian selected a new flying-off point, 32 miles to the north-west of Bango, 72 miles south of Miyako and 67 miles south-east of Ishigaki. Reducing the range to the two islands might increase the risk of an enemy air attack, but it potentially allowed more strikes to be launched throughout the day.

The air operations that Friday followed the now well-established pattern. First, shortly before dawn, a CAP screen of 13 Seafires was sent up to protect the Task Force. This was becoming increasingly tricky aboard *Indefatigable*, as 887 and 894 NAS were by then way below their established complement of fighters. Of the 40 Seafires embarked in the carrier at the start of Operation *Iceberg*, only 15 were left. The other 25 had either been lost or damaged beyond repair in accidents. Only 5 replacements had reached the carrier over the previous few weeks, and of the 20 available aircraft, several had mechanical problems which temporarily put them out of action. So, Capt. Graham and his crew were struggling to provide the fighters that the Task Force needed for its CAP. As a result, the weakened CAP screen was augmented by 6 Hellcats from *Indomitable*.

Also before dawn, four more Hellcats took off from *Indomitable*, to conduct a pre-strike reconnaissance of the two target islands. It was found that the Japanese had been busy over the past two days, and most of the craters had been filled in, so all six airfields were fully operational again. It was a frustrating discovery. The Avengers would have been better using smaller general-purpose bombs, designed to explode on contact with the ground. This meant that the Avenger crews had to bomb the runways all over again.

The Carrier Strike Force of TF 57 at anchor in San Pedro Bay, Leyte during the force's week-long sojourn there. In the foreground is HMS *Victorious*, with in line, HMS *Formidable*, the maintenance carrier HMS *Unicorn*, HMS *Indefatigable* and HMS *Indomitable* lying off her starboard quarter. HMS *Illustrious* is to the left.

Two strikes were launched against each island, with the main effort being the two larger airfields. Each strike was made up of an Avenger squadron of 12 to 14 bombers and a close escort of 16 Corsairs. By the end of these attacks, five of the six Sakishima airfields had been put out of action again. The exception was Hirara airfield on Miyako, where two of its three runways had only been partially cratered and so were still deemed operable by skilled pilots. Two more strikes were launched in the afternoon, this time by the rocket-armed Fireflies of 1770 NAS. The first strike targeted coastal shipping around the islands, in an effort to reduce the Japanese ability to move troops around and repair equipment, while the second hit ground installations on Miyako, where the Japanese AA defences were still considered very effective.

In addition, another 20 Corsairs made up the Target CAP, providing air cover over the entire Sakishima chain. During these patrols, signs that a new airfield was being constructed in woodland on the southern side of Iriomote Jima near the village of Taketomi was noted, and so the site was duly strafed, then photographed by Hellcats as part of the usual post-strike survey. This island, 10 miles to the west of Ishigaki Jima, was thought too rugged for any airfields. It was a less-than-ideal site, but still, during future operations, the British would make sure it never became operational. Finally, at 1710hrs, once the last of the Target CAP fighters had been recovered, tactical control of the Task Force was returned to Rawlings, who ordered the formation to turn about and set a course for Leyte.

The passage there was uneventful, and the Task Force finally dropped anchor off Leyte in the late morning of Monday 23 April. It had been 32 days since it had left Ulithi, at the start of its operational tour of duty off the Sakishimas. For the Royal Navy, it was something of a record. No British fleet had remained at sea on active operations for so long since the blockading squadrons off Napoleonic France, over two centuries before. After an all-too short hiatus at Leyte, the fleet would put to sea again, and repeat the whole process. At that stage though, Rawlings and his superior, Adm. Fraser in Sydney, were unsure what that would involve. The likelihood was that it would see them return to the Sakishimas to continue their attacks on the islands. However, there was also a strong possibility that they would be sent south to support the Australian-led assault on Borneo, which was due to begin in a week's time. For the moment though, most of the crew didn't care. They just enjoyed the chance to rest.

From Leyte to Miyako

During its visit to Leyte, the British Pacific Fleet was anchored in San Pedro Roads, on the south-west side of the island, far away from any port that a British sailor might recognize. In his report, Capt. Denny of *Victorious* described his crew's disappointment: 'It is feared

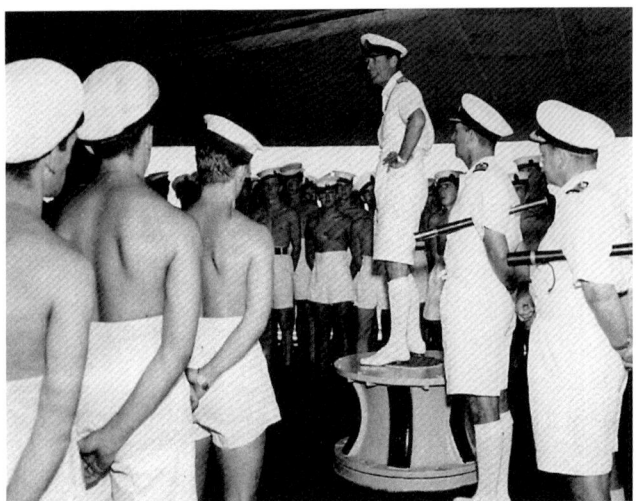

A 'pep talk' to young Canadian seamen by V. Adm. Sir Philip Vian, standing atop the capstan on the forecastle of HMCS *Uganda*, during the fleet's week-long sojourn in San Pedro Bay, Leyte. Vian was a believer in keeping his men motivated and informed, and often gave short speeches of this kind.

that the period in Leyte won't produce all the restoration of stamina and morale that might be expected.' He explained why. Like the other ships in the fleet, *Victorious* was anchored miles from the shore, with virtually no boats provided for shore leave. He described conditions aboard as 'pretty grim for the young air crews, still unaccustomed and imperfectly conditioned to shipboard life'. Denny felt that if the exhausted air crews were accommodated somewhere ashore, they would quickly be restored to the peak of efficiency. Unfortunately, this never happened, and the men of the Task Force had to make do with a week-long break from operations cocooned in their own ships.

This though, was less of a problem than it first appeared. Two Fighter Wings, 5 FW in *Indomitable* and 47 FW in *Victorious*, were either at or beyond the limits of their operational tours. It was evident that the young men who made up the air and ground crews of the fighter wings were showing signs of strain and fatigue. Frankly, so too were their aircraft, but they had to remain and be serviced *in situ*. So, Rawlings agreed to the airmen being sent back to Sydney, for rest, leave and then redeployment. Another Fighter Wing, 15 FW, embarked in *Illustrious*, had already exceeded its operational tour, and with the carrier needing repairs, those air crews and maintenance staff were also sent off to Australia. Of Vian's original air units, only the air wing of Fireflies and Seafires embarked in *Indefatigable* remained for the next phase of operations. So too did 6 FW, which was embarked in the newcomer *Victorious*.

That meant that when they were in Leyte, all three carriers received reinforcements to their Fighter Wings in the form of both men and aircraft. This was achieved by means of some reorganization. First, 1840 NAS embarked in the escort carrier *Speaker* was disbanded and

The fleet carrier HMS *Victorious*, pictured during TF 57's maintenance and replenishment visit to San Pedro Bay, Leyte in late April 1945. Ranged behind the more modern aircraft, just in front of the assembly of sailors on the flight deck is the Supermarine Walrus floatplane, a biplane used for Air-Sea Rescue (ASR) missions.

The Dido-class AA cruiser HMS *Euryalus* passing through the Suez Canal to join the BPF, in 1945. By then the cruiser had an enviable battle record, having played a major part in the Second Battle of Sirte (1942) and seen action during the landings on Sicily and at Salerno. *Euryalus* would prove to be a useful addition to TF 57.

transferred in its entirety to 1839 NAS in *Indomitable*. It then formed the core of the carriers' reconstructed Fighter Wing 5. *Speaker*'s place as the CAP provider during fleet replenishment was taken over by *Ruler*, which had the 18 Hellcats and 4 Avengers of 885 NAS embarked. Temporary repairs were still being carried out on *Illustrious*, which was anchored next to the maintenance carrier HMS *Unicorn*. The escort carriers as well as *Unicorn* were laden with replacement aircraft and air crews, and these were transferred to *Formidable*, *Indefatigable*, *Indomitable* and *Victorious*. This was done using lighters (barges), a process that took the best part of a week to complete.

There was little time for the relaxation or visits ashore the men wanted. At least two sailors though, managed to slip ashore in a barge, and found a bar in San Antonio on Samar, where they found the beer almost prohibitively expensive. For the main though, the crews were kept busy maintaining and repairing their ships and engaging in inter-ship events, such as boxing matches or rowing regattas. Harry Russell from Orkney, serving aboard *King George V*, remembered losing a ship-wide arm-wrestling contest to 'a blooming great gorilla of a stoker'! The ships took on stores of all kinds, and fresh personnel, all of whom had to be absorbed into their ship's company. The repair ships *Artifex* and *Resource* were also kept busy repairing the damage to *Indefatigable* from her kamikaze hit, while the crew of *Unicorn* did the same, trying to repair as many defective aircraft as it could. As a result, the number of operational Seafires embarked in *Indefatigable* was doubled in the space of a week.

Finally, on 28 April, Rawlings had his orders, transmitted from Adm. Nimitz by way of Adm. Fraser in Sydney. The Task Force would continue with the Sakishima operation, and the neutralization of the Japanese airfields there. Two days later, on Monday 30 April, the cycle of replenishment, storing and repair had been completed. At 0700hrs that morning, a tanker group and its escorts had sailed from Leyte, to take up station in the refuelling rendezvous. The following morning, at 0630hrs, the warships of TF 57 raised their anchors and headed out to sea. The shape of the Task Force had altered slightly. First, *Formidable* had officially replaced *Illustrious* as the carrier group's fourth carrier. *Argonaut* had been detached to undergo a refit, as had the destroyers *Wager* and *Whelp*. The cruiser was replaced by the Canadian light cruiser *Uganda* and the AA cruiser *Euryalus*. The destroyers *Ulster*, *Urchin* and *Ursa* had already been detached and had been replaced by *Kempenfelt*, *Quilliam*, *Wessex* and *Whirlwind*, four of them drawn from Task Force 112, the Fleet Train.

The embarked Air Wings of the four carriers were up to strength again. Damaged or defective aircraft had been repaired and losses had been made good. This time though, many

Royal Naval air and naval operations around Miyako Jima, 4 May, 1945

On Friday 4 May, V. Adm. Rawlings planned to devote most of his fleet's efforts to the pounding of Miyako Jima by both air and sea. By dawn, TF 57 was at Flying-off Point Bango 75 miles south of the island. After a dawn reconnaissance of both Ishigaki and Miyako, two air strikes were launched two hours apart, one targeting each island.

IRABU

SHIMOJIJI

Key:
- Heavy AA guns
- Wireless station
- Radar station
- Seaplane base
- Barracks

KURIMA

Key:

Fleet Air Arm

Task Force 57 at Launch-off Point Bango, 65nmi to south-east

Air strike (Strike leader: Lt. Cdr. Hay): 24 Avengers (six each from 820, 848, 849 & 857 NAS)

14 Corsairs (seven each from 1836 & 1842 NAS)

7 Fireflies (from 1770 NAS)

'TarCAP' (Combat Air Patrol over Target): 16 Corsairs (eight each from 1834 & 1841 NAS)

'TG 57.1 CAP' Bombardment Force Combat Air Patrol: 6 Corsairs (from 1842 NAS)

'TG57.1 Spot' Naval Bombardment Spotter Aircraft: 3 Corsairs

(one from 1836, one from 1841 NAS)

Royal Navy

Bombardment Force (Vice Admiral Rawlings)

Battleships: *King George V* (flagship), *Howe*

Cruisers: *Black Prince, Euryalus, Gambia, Swiftsure, Uganda*

and six destroyers

Japanese airfield defence

Herara: 126 heavy (75mm) AA guns

27 light (25mm) twin AA guns

Nobara: 12 light (25mm) twin AA guns

Sukama: 6 light (25mm) twin AA guns

Air Early Warning Radar station at Cape Higashi-Hennazaki protected by two light (25mm) twin AA guns

Seaplane base north of Sunayama Bay: 4 light (25mm) twin AA guns

Location: Sakishima Islands, 150nmi south-west of Okinawa
Light, scattered cloud cover, 3/10ths at 6,000ft
Wind North-West, 12kts
Visibility: Excellent – Over 12nmi

EVENTS

1. 0530hrs. A reconnaissance of Miyako reveals that the airfield has been repaired since the last strike two weeks before, and there is a high level of air activity on its three airfields.

2. 0540hrs. A CAP of Seafires and Hellcats takes off to protect the TF. Considerable enemy air activity is detected on radar over Miyako. A second CAP force of 16 Corsairs is sent to patrol the skies over Miyako. It arrives at 0635hrs.

3. 0640hrs. An air strike made up of 24 Avenger bombers and seven Fireflies launched 35mins earlier makes landfall to the south-south-west of Miyako. It divides into two groups.

4. 0646hrs. Strike Force 'Charlie' bombs Nobara airfield, then turns south-east, and returns to the carriers.

5. 0647hrs. Strike Forces 'Able' and 'Baker' bomb Hirara airfield, each approaching from a different direction. On completion the aircraft withdraw to the south-east.

6. 0647hrs. Fireflies conduct rocket attacks of airfield buildings and installations at Hirara, while half of the escorting Corsairs carry out strafing runs over the airfield's AA defences.

7. 0655hrs–0710hrs. After forming up to the south of Cape Higashi-Hennazaki, the strike force returns to the TF. By 0810hrs, all aircraft have landed back on their carriers.

8. 1131hrs. Seventy miles to the south of Miyako, the carriers of the TF come under sustained attack from Japanese kamikaze aircraft.

9. 1140hrs. The naval Bombardment Force approaches the southern coast of Miyako. A CAP of six Corsairs patrol overhead.

10. 1205hrs. The bombardment commences, with the battleships *King George V* and *Howe* targeting Hirara airfield, while the five cruisers shell Nobara and Sukuma.

11. 1205hrs. Three Corsairs from *Indomitable* and *Victorious* act as spotting aircraft, correcting the fall of shot of the Bombardment Force. This greatly assists the accuracy of the bombardment.

12. 1247hrs. Rawlings ceases fire, and the Bombardment Force returns at speed to rejoin the TF, and bolster its defences.

13. 1320hrs. The remaining TarCAP over Miyako is withdrawn, and ordered to return to its carriers. The Flight Controller aboard *Indomitable* guides the aircraft home. Aircraft from *Formidable*, whose flight deck is out of action, are directed to land on other carriers.

of the air crews would lack the combat experience of their predecessors – the air crews which had spent a month attacking the Sakishima Islands. Still, at least they'd be fresh and ready for what lay ahead. At dawn, on Thursday 3 May, TF 57 rendezvoused with its tankers at Rendezvous Area Mosquito. The refuelling of the fleet was completed by 1530hrs. Then Rawlings ordered them north, towards Flying-off Point Bomba, to the south of Ishigaki. His orders laid out three aims for the forthcoming operation:

1. To render the airfields of the Sakishima Gunto unserviceable.
2. To conduct an offensive against flak positions there, and for surface units to assist the cratering of runways by conducting shore bombardment.
3. To maintain a CAP screen over the islands.

The plan for Friday 4 May was the deployment of a CAP patrol over Miyako, followed by the bombardment of the three airfields on the island and the AA batteries protecting them. A secondary strike would also be launched at Ishigaki. This time the flying-off point favoured by Vian on 20 April was used again (23° 44' North, 125° 11' East). The CAP over the Task Force was flown off at 0530hrs, made up of 16 Seafires. Ten minutes later, bogeys were detected to the north of the island, heading east towards Okinawa. Undoubtedly, they were on their way to attack the US Fifth Fleet. A group of Japanese fighters passing slightly to the south of Ishigaki sighted the British Task Force, and turned towards it. They though, were driven off by the CAP screen, some 30 miles north of the carriers, and a Zeke was shot down. At 0700hrs, a Target CAP was set to patrol over Miyako, which would serve as a tripwire if any further attempts were made to attack the Task Force.

At 0605hrs the first bomber strike was launched, comprising 24 Avengers and 20 escorting fighters. The attack was a success – no aircraft were lost, and Hirara, Sukuma and Nobara were all cratered. The top-cover fighters also managed to conduct a Ramrod attack, strafing the Hirara AA defences. At 0815hrs, the second strike was launched, which was of a similar size to the earlier one. This headed west towards Ishigaki, but on getting there both Ishigaki Main and Hegina were found to still be cratered, following the air attacks by Task Force 52's US escort carriers. The air attack added to these craters, while also putting the Miyara airfield out of action. However, the AA batteries on both islands remained vigilant, and opened heavy fire at the attackers, without achieving any serious hits. The bombs released, the strike aircraft then returned to their carriers.

During these attacks, only one enemy aircraft attempted to fly towards the Task Force. At 0827hrs a bogey was detected on the air warning radar of *Indefatigable*. The contact was approaching the Task Force from the west. However, it turned away before it came within visual sighting range of the Task Force CAP. The likelihood is that it was some kind of reconnaissance plane sweeping the waters south of Ishigaki. Meanwhile, at 0820hrs, after the second air strike had been launched, the Task Force left its flying-off point and headed north, closing with the coast of Miyako. This was a prelude to the bombardment of the island by the Task Force's large surface warships.

At 1000hrs, the Task Force divided while still 47 miles south of Miyako. The Bombardment Group was led by the fleet flagship *King George V*, accompanied by *Howe*. Accompanying the two battleships were five cruisers: *Euryalus* and *Black Prince* on the port bow of the capital ships, and *Swiftsure*, *Gambia* and *Uganda* in a line ahead formation off the flagship's port quarter. They then closed with the coast at 24kts. Dividing the fleet like this was a gamble for Rawlings, as it considerably weakened the AA firepower of the combined Task Force and left each group vulnerable to air attack. Rawlings though, considered that the destructive power of a bombardment of Hirara and the island's other two airfields greatly outweighed the risk of a large-scale kamikaze attack developing. He had realized that only a large-scale naval bombardment would put the Japanese airfields out of action for more than just a few days. Also, up until this point, all of the major kamikaze attacks had been directed at the US fleet off Okinawa.

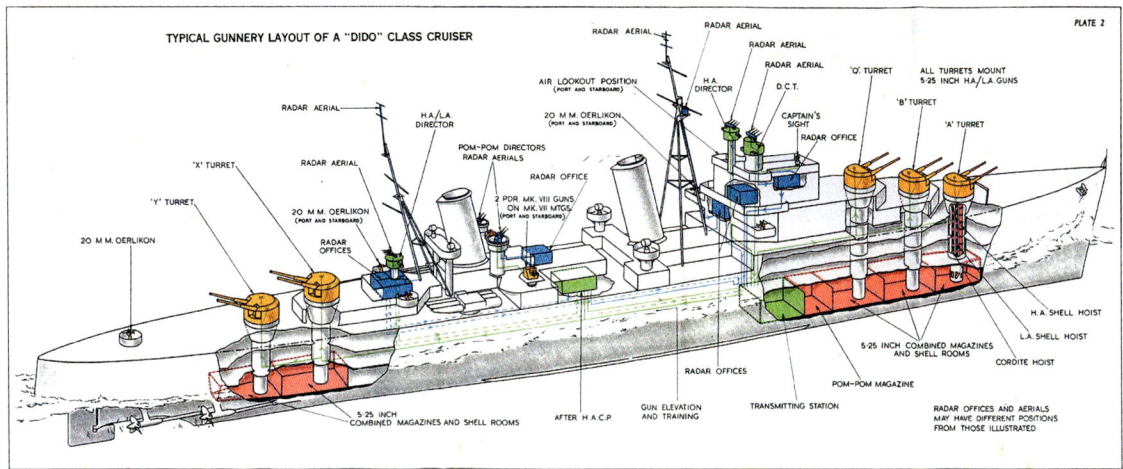

As the Bombardment Force continued on towards the island, the Carrier Group remained in place, 45 miles south of Miyako. Both Task Groups were now protected by their own CAP screen, which Vian had reinforced with additional Hellcats. The bombardment was scheduled to begin at noon. Before it did, three Corsairs were sent aloft from *Formidable* and attached to the Target CAP to act as spotters for the Bombardment Force, one covering Hirara, and the others observing fire on the two secondary airfields. At 1155hrs, the fleet flagship reached the commencement point (24° 35.5' North, 125° 10' East), 10 miles off the coast and 14½ miles south-west of Hirara airfield. The warships steered inshore, on a course of 070°, making 15kts, the cruisers now 3 miles further inshore than the battleships. That meant that all of their guns could bear on Hirara, and the cruisers were just in range.

Rawlings gave the order to open fire at 1205hrs. The AA cruisers *Black Prince* and *Euryalus* fired air-burst shells from their 5.25in guns over Nobara, while the 14in battleships fired at Hirara. Once the air-burst bombardment was over, *Swiftsure* and *Gambia* opened up on Nobara with their 6in guns, while the 6in guns of *Uganda* pounded Sukuma. Guided by the airborne spotters, this fire proved deadly accurate. At 1245hrs, Rawlings ordered the Bombardment Force to cease fire, and it turned away to rejoin the Carrier Group. In all, 195 14in rounds were fired at Hirara, while the cruisers between them fired 598 6in and 378 5.25in rounds at Nobara and Sukuma. The airborne observers reported that the runways were utterly devastated, while the airfields' AA defences and buildings had also been pounded hard. It would take quite a while for the Japanese to recover from this bombardment.

Meanwhile, the Carrier Group had come under air attack. At 1100hrs, four small groups of bogeys were detected approaching from the west, each of four or five enemy fighters. This came at just the wrong time for the British, when the powerful defensive formation had been denuded by the departure of the fleet's most powerful warships. Rawlings' decision, while fully justified by the success of the bombardment, had potentially serious consequences. While four groups continued to approach the Carrier Group from the west, another group began edging around to the south. The CAP fighters reacted by dividing between the two threats. These Japanese flight-sized groups proved to be the decoys, and most withdrew as soon as they were engaged by the British fighters.

However, at 1131hrs, a hitherto undetected group of Japanese Zekes appeared directly above the carriers. The likelihood is that they had been flying at sea level, below the radar, and had circled around to the south and then to the east of the British carriers. Then, when about a dozen or so miles from their target they climbed steeply, to a height where they could launch dive bomb attacks. The air search radars on the carriers had been so focused on the threat from the west and south that the operators hadn't spotted the aircraft approaching

Probably the most efficient anti-air protection in TF *57* was provided by its three AA cruisers *Argonaut*, *Black Prince* and *Hermione*. These Dido-class AA cruisers mounted ten 5.25in guns in five twin turrets, which were linked to the ship's powerful fire control and air warning radars. For close-range AA defence, the Didos mounted 2-pdr pom-poms and 20mm oerlikons.

HMS *Formidable*, shortly after the carrier was struck by a kamikaze fighter on 4 May. As well as damaging the island, the explosion of the Zeke and its bomb blew a hole in the flight deck and dented it. This damage was patched with quick-setting concrete, allowing flying operations to resume.

from the opposite direction. The first time the four Zekes were spotted was when one was seen diving steeply out of the clouds, at a height of 3,000ft, and heading directly towards *Formidable* from astern. It was clearly a kamikaze attack.

The AA guns of the Carrier Group opened up and Vian ordered his force to make high-speed emergency turns, in an attempt to throw off the aim of the Japanese pilots. It worked, as the diving Zeke pulled up at the last minute as it was overshooting the carrier, but managed to strafe the flight deck as it passed. It was hit and was seen to be on fire. Both the carrier and the kamikaze plane turned sharply to starboard, but the fighter had the tighter turn, and as it circled around it lined up on the carrier's flight deck. A second before impact, it released a 250kg bomb. Then the kamikaze plane struck the flight deck abreast of the island. The resulting explosion ripped the Japanese fighter apart, but it also caused havoc on the carrier's flight deck, sending a sheet of flame skyward, reaching as high as the top of the carrier's funnel.

Ten minutes before, *Formidable* had flown off the three Corsairs earmarked as spotters for the Bombardment Force. That done, the deck handlers were busy moving a squadron of recently landed Avengers forward in order to clear the landing area aft for any more returning aircraft. Eight crewmen were killed outright in the explosion, and another 47 wounded – most of them deck handlers. Eleven of the Avengers were wrecked. The explosion blew a 2ft-diameter hole in the flight deck, and dented the surrounding armoured deck by up to 2ft for

The Japanese fighter struck the starboard side of *Indomitable*'s flight deck, but it then bounced owing to the flat angle of approach, before leaping over the port side of the carrier into the sea. It then exploded, without harming anyone but the kamikaze pilot. The destroyers HMS *Quilliam* (left) and HMAS *Quickmatch* (foreground) both fired at the aircraft as it made its final dive.

several feet around the hole. Worse still, a steel splinter from the deck was blown downwards into the carrier's central boiler room, piercing a fuel tank and steam pipes before lodging in the carrier's inner bottom.

The carrier's experienced damage-control teams reacted immediately, putting out the fire on the flight deck and rescuing the wounded. The wreckage was then bulldozed over the ship's side. The damage in the boiler room led to a temporary loss of speed to 16kts, but the teams worked hard to repair the damage and clear up the mess. By 1254hrs, just 80 minutes after the kamikaze strike, *Formidable* was capable of making 24kts. By 1700hrs, the flight deck was operational again. This though, wasn't the end of the kamikazes.

Three minutes after that first hit, another Zeke was spotted over the Carrier Group, diving out of the clouds at 3,000ft. It began a steep dive towards *Indomitable*, which was turning wildly to avoid the plunging kamikaze. The carrier's AA guns were also firing, and at what seemed like the last moment a 40mm Bofors shell hit the Zeke, which was seen to flatten out of its dive at the last moment, with flames pouring from its engine. The Japanese fighter hit the flight deck, almost as if crash landing, then continued on, bouncing over the ship's side and into the sea. The bomb the Zeke carried exploded harmlessly in the water, and the plane was torn apart. The only damage suffered by Vian's flagship was to one of her Type 282 fire control radar aerials. The trail of aircraft wreckage left on the flight deck was quickly dealt with, although some bits were kept as souvenirs.

Five minutes later, at 1142hrs, a third Zeke appeared, and began a dive towards *Indomitable*. Once again the carrier's close-range weapons opened up, and the kamikaze aircraft was hit repeatedly as it dived towards the carrier. All the while the ship was turning hard to avoid the blazing plane. The Zeke crashed into the sea, just 10yds off the carrier's starboard bow, and exploded when it struck the water. Some 20 minutes later, shortly after noon, two more kamikazes from the same group made their appearance, but were shot down by fire from the carriers – one kill each claimed by the AA gunners of *Indomitable* and *Indefatigable*.

The same kamikaze as the one shown in the bottom photo on the previous page, moments after hitting the sea off the port bow of *Indomitable* from the carrier's island. The resulting explosion can be seen behind the carrier's port-side forward battery of 4.5in AA guns.

So, the kamikaze attack on the Carrier Group ended at about the same time as Rawlings' Bombardment Force began pounding the airfields on Miyako. By then, word of the kamikaze attack had reached the fleet commander. So, as soon as the bombardment finished, the Bombardment Force raced back to the south, making 24kts. By 1420hrs it was close enough to be able to support the carriers with their air search radars and AA guns. Rawlings ordered the two forces to merge, and to form up into Cruising Formation 5B, a tight defensive cordon that made the most of the fleet's combined anti-aircraft firepower.

During the afternoon, a number of small groups of Japanese aircraft tried to approach the Task Force, but all of them were detected on radar and the CAP screen managed to intercept the enemy aircraft some 20 to 30 miles to the west of the British ships. The last of these attempted attacks took place at 1720hrs, but again the Japanese formation was broken up by the reinforced CAP screen, and the Japanese planes were either shot down or driven off. Just over half an hour later, at 1755hrs, Rawlings ordered the Task Force to withdraw towards the south-west for the night. Sunset that evening was at 1911hrs, by which time the British ships were clear of the coast. The tally in terms of aircraft shot down was 14 – three by AA fire from the warships and 11 more by the CAP. This though, was balanced against the loss of 11 Avengers on *Victorious* – a significant part of the Carrier Group's bomber force.

At 0120hrs on Saturday 5 May, repairs to *Formidable*'s central boiler room were completed, and once again the carrier could steam at full speed. Vian felt this was vital if she was to return to the fray off the Sakishimas. During the night, the Task Force returned to its old flying-off point south of Miyako. At dawn (0600hrs), the usual CAP screens were sent up, over both islands, protecting the Task Force as well. There was no sign of enemy air activity, and a reconnaissance of Miyako showed that there was virtually no AA fire coming from the islands. This was a relief to the air crews waiting to launch their daily strikes, and confirmation that the naval bombardment of the previous day had been a real success. The reconnaissance also looked at the nascent airstrip on Iriomote, but it appeared that no further work had been carried out there.

At 0730hrs, a bogey was detected some 59 miles away to the west, heading towards the Task Force. A flight of Corsairs on CAP duty was sent off to intercept it, guided towards its target by the flight controller aboard *Indomitable*. The flight was from *Formidable*'s 1841 NAS, which had been operating temporarily from *Victorious*. The bogey turned out to be a twin-engined Dinah on a reconnaissance flight. When its crew spotted the Corsairs, it turned away to the north-west, but the Japanese aircraft was pursued by two Corsairs, and was eventually shot down to the north of Formosa after a lengthy chase of almost 300 miles. It was revealing that no other enemy aircraft were encountered in the air that Saturday. This suggested a reduction in Japanese activity – or a lull pending another large-scale attack.

Meanwhile, two morning strikes were launched at 0630hrs, with one targeting each of the main islands. These were each made up of 16 Avengers and 12 Corsairs and Hellcats.

On 4 May, HMS *Indomitable* was attacked by a kamikaze Zeke, whose pilot misjudged his approach as the carrier turned. This shows the final moments of the dive, with the kamikaze circled. The attack was watched by Sub. Lt Mackie, who was in the Avenger parked at the stern of the flight deck, directly underneath the circled fighter.

By late morning, the aircraft had all returned safely and reported that all six airfields were completely inoperable. The lack of Japanese flak over Miyako delighted the air crews, and it was clear when flying over the island that all three airfields had been heavily pounded by the bombardment of the previous day. Hirara, in particular, was in ruins, and the runway so heavily damaged that the airmen were hard placed to see how it could be repaired without a major engineering effort. The escorts took advantage of the lack of enemy fire to strafe the Japanese barracks on the island.

At 1630 hrs on Saturday afternoon, the Task Force headed away to the south-east and began preparing for a refuelling rendezvous the following day. This was carried out on 6 and 7 May at Cootie. In the meantime, the US Support Carrier Group, TG 52.1, took over the task of pounding the Sakishima airfields. Aboard *Formidable*, repair parties temporarily dealt with the depression in the armoured flight deck by levelling it with quick-drying cement. As a result, *Formidable* was deemed fully operational again, and her CAP and gunfire-spotting aircraft, which had temporarily been housed in other carriers, were landed back aboard their home carrier. The wounded from the Japanese attack of 4 May were transferred to the escort carrier *Speaker*, which would take them to Leyte, where the hospital ship *Oxfordshire* was waiting for them. The replenishment went smoothly and was completed on schedule on 7 May. At 1400hrs, the Task Force sailed back to its usual position off the Sakishimas.

The main runway of Ishigaki Main airfield, on Ishigaki Jima, on 5 May, the day after the first kamikaze strike on TF 57. This image, time-stamped at 1459hrs, was one of the many post-strike reconnaissance photographs taken in the aftermath of bombing strikes.

The return of the kamikazes

On the evening of 7 May, the British crews were delighted by the news that Germany had surrendered unconditionally, and that the body of Adolf Hitler had been found in Berlin. The war in Europe was finally over, and their families back home were now safe. All that remained was to bring the war against Japan to an equally satisfying conclusion. In Britain, the United States and the Soviet Union, Tuesday 8 May was VE-Day – a cause for mass celebration. In Task Force 57 though, apart from 'splicing the mainbrace' that evening – the issuing of an extra rum ration – it was just another day on the Pacific front line. Rawlings had planned another shore bombardment that morning, this time off Ishigaki, but poor weather led to the operation being cancelled. He and Vian had learned their lesson from 4 May, and this time the two groups would remain close enough together to aid each other if another kamikaze attack materialized. The low cloud and frequent rain squalls though, also led to a cancellation of flying operations, and so TF 57 withdrew again for the night.

However, by dawn on Wednesday 9 May, TF 57 was in a new flying-off point, 38 miles north of Bango, 64 miles due south from Miyako and 85 miles south-east of Ishigaki. That day, four Avenger bombing strikes were scheduled, with two targeting each island. The early morning reconnaissance flight revealed that the runways at Hirara had been repaired, so the airfield would receive extra attention. The first strike was flown off at 0830hrs, and the other three followed at 20-minute intervals. The second strike targeted Ishigaki, while the

Bomb-armed Avengers of 857 NAS, from *Indomitable*, waiting to begin their attack on Ishigaki Main airfield on the morning of 9 May. In the background, other Avengers from 849 NAS, from *Victorious*, have already dropped their bombs over the runway, which is wreathed in white coral-flecked smoke.

rest attacked Miyako, two of them concentrating on Hirara. The usual CAP patrols were also sent up over the two islands as well as the Task Force.

That morning, apart from the still unsettled overcast, with cloud creeping in, all seemed to go well. While some work had been done repairing all of the Sakishima runways, after the day's strikes all of them were rendered inoperable again, including Hirara. One bomb dropped by an Avenger caused an impressively large crater – presumably striking a previously bombed patch on the runway. The air crews also noted just how battered the six airfields and runways were now looking. Over Ishigaki, when the runways were rendered inoperable, the last flights of Avengers switched their attention to other targets such as barracks and vehicle parks. Corsairs on CAP patrol over the island also spotted an Aichi D-3A Val dive bomber parked just inside the entrance to a cave. It was destroyed by a Hellfire, flying in at low level and firing tracer into the cave.

However, while the British had been bombing the islands, the Japanese had been concentrating on the British Task Force. At 1145hrs an enemy reconnaissance aircraft was spotted on radar, but it escaped when the CAP Seafires closed with it. This though, meant that the Japanese knew where the Task Force was. At 1645hrs, several bogeys were detected 28 miles away, approaching from the west. They were coming in fast and at low altitude. The CAP Seafires were vectored out to intercept them as far from the Task Force as possible. Some of the aircraft turned out to be decoys, which withdrew when the British fighters approached them. Others though were clearly kamikazes. The CAP screen wasn't foolproof – three Seafires targeted a single kamikaze Zeke, and although they shot it down, three others slipped past the screen and headed towards the Task Force just above sea level. As Vian wryly noted of the incident later, 'Their foolishness ... was to cost the fleet dear.'

The other three Zekes sidestepped a second group of Seafires, and then climbed quickly out of sight into the low clouds at 3,000ft, before beginning their dives towards the British carriers. At 1651hrs, one of them dived towards *Victorious*, and Capt. Denny began turning the carrier at speed, then swinging it the other way once the kamikaze had committed itself to its final dive. It wasn't quite enough. Although the carrier's gunners hit the Zeke repeatedly, it kept coming, and struck the carrier's flight deck near the forward lift. As it struck, its

A Supermarine Seafire of 887 NAS has been ranged onto its spot on the flight deck of HMS *Implacable*, ready for a sortie, and the flight deck crew are busily lowering the fighter's wings. This was done hydraulically for US-built fighters, but with the Seafire this was done manually.

bomb detonated, to add to the chaos. The blast blew a hole in the armoured flight deck and knocked out the lift motor, putting it out of action. The carrier's only working catapult was also destroyed, and a 4.5in AA gun turret put out of action. The fire control teams were still dealing with the blaze when the carrier was hit again.

This time the kamikaze had been approaching the carrier from astern, in a shallower glide, but had been hit repeatedly. Somehow though, the pilot managed to power glide on towards the carrier, while his plane, another Zeke, blazed furiously around him. At 1656hrs, it struck the after-flight deck, but this time the kamikaze plane skidded across the deck, smashing through three Corsairs, before plunging over the ship's side, wrecking a gun director and some arrestor wires as it went. Again, the fire control teams fought to deal with the blaze, while the flight deck crew began clearing the wreckage.

A minute later, at 1657hrs, a third attacker was seen diving towards *Victorious* from astern. Capt. Denny though, handled his carrier well. Afterwards he wrote; '*Victorious* was an immensely handy ship to handle, with a big rudder. I could spin her around quite rapidly, and I managed to ruin both my kamikaze attacks.' The carrier turned at the last minute, ruining the enemy's approach. So, the Zeke pilot revved his engine, despite being peppered by hits from the carrier, and shifted his attention to the battleship *Howe*, a mile ahead of the carrier. The battleship began turning hard to starboard, and the kamikaze, by then on fire, was hit repeatedly as it made its final shallow approach. In the end, it roared harmlessly over *Howe*'s quarterdeck and crashed into the sea 100yds away in a spectacular fireball.

The final kamikaze attack of the day came at 1705hrs. Once it dived out of the clouds the Zeke began diving towards the stern of *Formidable*, before seemingly switching to *Indomitable*. The fighter seemed to lead a charmed life, as the combined AA fire of the two

In this kamikaze attack on HMS *Victorious* at 1656hrs on 9 May, the hard turn of Capt. Denny's carrier threw off the Zeke pilot. He misjudged the final approach, pancaking into the deck before scraping across the flight deck and over the port side of the carrier into the sea, landing 200yds off the vessel's port bow. The moment is captured from *Indomitable*, a mile away.

carriers struggled to keep up with the pilot's jinking from side to side. This also threw off Capt. Andrewes of *Formidable* and Capt. Eccles of *Indomitable*, who, like Capt. Denny, twisted and turned to throw off the kamikaze pilot. At the last second though, the Zeke turned towards *Formidable* and crashed into the carrier's after deck park of fighters. The resulting fireball led to onlookers fearing the worst, especially when it was followed by a dense column of smoke. The explosion had caused a fire to break out among the wreckage of these Corsairs, but otherwise the carrier was surprisingly undamaged. At a stroke though, *Formidable* had lost 18 of her fighters. By 1755hrs, Capt. Andrewes signalled Vian, to report that his carrier was back in operation. The British casualties that afternoon were also surprisingly light – three crew killed on *Victorious* and one more on *Formidable*.

At 1950hrs, having regained tactical control from Vian, Rawlings withdrew his fleet towards Rendezvous Area Cootie to refuel and to finish any temporary repairs. In the meantime, US Task Group 52.1 had been diverted to take the British Task Force's place south of the Sakishimas. It had been a trying day for the British crews. Aboard the two damaged carriers, repair parties worked through the night to repair what damage they could, before making more extensive repairs during the coming replenishment. Vian though, took heart from the comment made by an American Liaison Officer aboard *Indomitable*. He noted that if a US wooden-decked carrier had been struck in the way *Victorious* and *Formidable* had been, then it would probably have been lost.

The final phase

On the morning of Thursday 10 May, TF 57 rendezvoused with four tankers and two escort carriers of the Fleet Train and began refuelling. Repairs continued while *Ruler* provided CAP cover overhead. During the refuelling, Rawlings, Vian and their staffs had come up with some tactical improvements to counter the kamikazes. First, the radar pickets would be resumed, this time with two pairs of cruisers and destroyers sited 12 miles out from the Task Force, to the north-west and the south-west. That should improve radar coverage. Each pair would have its own CAP cover of four fighters, with the provision to quickly reinforce these if they appeared to be under threat. Next, the Dido-class AA cruisers would be redeployed closer to the carriers, which themselves would be grouped closer together, around

a 2,000yd circle of the Task Force's centre point – the guide cruiser. Finally, a destroyer was stationed immediately astern of each carrier, to increase its AA cover – this appeared to be the preferred line of approach for the kamikaze pilots. When flying resumed, all these tactical modifications were in place.

When TF 57 resumed flying operations off the Sakishimas on Saturday 12 May, the flying-off point was moved 18 miles further east, to reduce the risk of detection. This seemed to work, as the Task Force was spared from Japanese attention. It was clear to Rawlings that their time off the Sakishima Islands was ending. His carriers needed proper repairs and many of his other warships were developing defects after so long at sea. In addition, the makeshift Fleet Train was struggling to maintain its hitherto highly efficient support of the British warships. An exchange of signals with Adms Fraser, Nimitz and Spruance led to the decision that the British Pacific Fleet would cease offensive operations in just under two weeks' time, on 25 May.

From 12 May on, in light of the recent kamikaze attacks, TF 57 adopted a new cruising formation, 5F. This, essentially, incorporated all of the redisposition sketched out by Rawlings and Vian – the carriers would be stationed a mile from the formation's central point, marked by the guide cruiser, and the battleships and cruisers would be stationed 500yds further out. Each carrier would be followed by a destroyer, while the other destroyers would form an outer ring, 4 miles from the guide cruiser. The whole idea was to provide the carriers with the best possible AA protection. That Saturday, flying operations followed the same pattern as before – only the targets would change, depending on weather conditions and information gleaned from early morning reconnaissance flights over Ishigaki and Miyako.

On the morning of 11 May the Essex-class carrier USS *Bunker Hill*, flagship of TF 58, was operating off Okinawa when it came under kamikaze attack. The carrier was struck by two of them, the first wrecking parked aircraft and dropping a bomb which exploded in the hangar. Thirty seconds later, the second kamikaze struck the base of the island and blew up, as did its bomb. Over 400 lives were lost in the attack, and the carrier was put out of commission for the remainder of the war. This emphasized the vulnerability of the US carriers' wooden decks.

Adm. Raymond A. Spruance USN (1886–1969) commanded the US Fifth Fleet ('The Big Blue Navy') during the Okinawa campaign, which including the Royal Navy's TF 57. Spruance, whose tactics ensured victory in the Battle of the Philippine Sea (1944), was a superb commander, who inspired his men, even in the face of the ferocious kamikaze onslaught they withstood off Okinawa.

The first of four planned strikes that Saturday took off at 0540hrs, an hour before sunrise. The intention was for it and a second afternoon strike to attack Ishigaki, and the two other strikes to target Miyako. However, the second strike on Ishigaki was cancelled due to the weather. Only serviceable airfields on Ishigaki, Ishigaki Main and Miyara, were successfully re-cratered by the first strike. It was the same on Miyako – Nobara and one runway at Hirara had been repaired, and these were both put out of action. The following strike then, targeted flak batteries, and a direct hit wiped out a troublesome 100mm AA battery at Hirara. Sunset that Saturday was at 1915hrs. That was when the radar pickets were recalled and the last of the CAP fighters were recovered, before the fleet withdrew to the south.

On Sunday morning, 13 May, three strikes were launched at Miyako and one at Ishigaki. At Hirara on Miyako, a new dispersal bay protected by earthen revetments was being built, and this was pounded hard. The runways, already unserviceable, were cratered even more. A particularly satisfying target was three barges, anchored in Yonaha Bay near Hirara, which were shot up. On Ishigaki, the three airfields hadn't been repaired during the night, so while half the 16 Avenger strike re-cratered them, the other bombers concentrated on airfield installations and oil storage areas which hadn't been as extensively damaged as those on Miyako. One of them, a radio station, was severely damaged and set ablaze. This, it was felt, would reduce coordination between the two islands and the airfields in Formosa. That night, the Task Force withdrew to Rendezvous Area Cootie, as US TG 52.3 provided locum cover for the British.

Over the next two days air ordnance was transferred as well as fuel and supplies, and the destroyers *Nepal*, *Troubridge* and *Tenacious* joined the Task Force. However, by dawn on Wednesday 16 May, TF 57 was back in position to the south-south-east of Miyako. Again, the same well-established pattern continued. Air strikes of 12–16 bomb-armed Avengers and 10–12 Corsairs were launched, three against Miyako and one targeting Ishigaki. By the end of the strikes, all airfields on the two islands were inoperable. The Japanese enthusiasm to repair them seems to have waned slightly, as nocturnal runway-repairing seemed to have slowed its pace. On the following day, Thursday 17 June, the Task Force was back on station by 0530hrs, but a lack of wind made flying operations problematic.

The carriers needed to steam at speed into the wind to increase air flow over the deck, in order to assist take-offs. With virtually no wind, sending fully armed aircraft aloft became a tricky business. Engine problems in *Indomitable* made high-speed manoeuvring impossible, while *Victorious*' damaged flight deck was still uneven, making flying operations hazardous until the carrier could be repaired. Still, this was partly solved by moving 20 of her aircraft to other carriers. Despite these problems, two small raids, each consisting of 10 bombers were launched at Miyako that day, and one more at Ishigaki. Apart from Miyara, all airfields were deemed out of action by the end of the day's operations. For the first time, the second Miyako strike targeted civilian targets, albeit ones which had been extensively requisitioned by the Japanese. So, bombs were dropped over the town and harbour of Hirara, to the west of the airfield.

The southern approaches to Hirara town on Miyako Jima, as the Avengers target barracks, vehicle parks and other military targets around the town, rather than the already well-pounded airfield nearby. Inevitably, casualties were suffered by the island's Japanese civilian population during these raids.

The Task Force withdrew again to refuel that evening and rendezvoused with the three tankers of the Fleet Train at Cootie the following morning, Friday 18 May. However, that morning disaster struck aboard *Formidable*. In the hangar, a Corsair accidentally fired its guns at an Avenger struck down ahead of her, and the bomber blew up. A major fire erupted, whose spread was helped by the fire curtains having been damaged earlier. Firefighting teams did what they could, but by noon, when the blaze was deemed out of control, the flames were doused by drenching the hangar with Foamite, a dense carbon-dioxide foam mix, that extinguished the blaze, at the cost of wrecking what few aircraft remained undamaged. In the end, *Formidable* lost 21 Corsairs and 7 Avengers.

By Friday evening, the carrier was deemed operational again, for what it was worth. For all practical purposes though, *Formidable*, with her reduced air complement, was practically useless for further strike operations. However, some replacement aircraft were transferred from the escort carriers *Chaser* and *Ruler*. At the same time, *Nepal* and *Parret* were detached to support the Fleet Train, which, consequently, lacked airborne anti-submarine protection. On Saturday afternoon, the Task Force headed north again amid worsening weather.

On reaching its usual flying-off point on Sunday 20 May, sunrise revealed the sea blanketed by thick fog. It was in these conditions that the shadowing destroyer *Quilliam* collided with the stern of Vian's flagship *Indomitable*. The carrier was barely scratched, but the destroyer had to be towed to Cootie, where the tug *Weasel* attached to the Fleet Train would take *Quilliam* to Leyte for repairs. For the voyage south, *Quilliam* was escorted by the AA cruiser *Black Prince* and the destroyer *Norman*, which provided *Quilliam* with the tow.

A gap in the fog at 0745hrs allowed a single strike to take off, rather than the four which had been planned. It proved hard to even find the island, but eventually the strike leader

Hirara airfield, from a fighter piloted by Maj. Hay, RM, who often acted as a strike leader during the campaign, and who orchestrated the bombing mission from a vantage point above the target, while also coordinating the escorting fighters.

spotted Hirara through the cloud and led a bombing attack on the town. This was followed by a low-level attack by 8 Fireflies of 1770 NAS, detached from the escort, which strafed the town's harbour. The strike managed to return successfully to the Task Force, thanks to radar guidance and a fair slice of luck.

Shortly after noon, Rawlings received a signal from Adm. Fraser, passing on a request from Spruance for the British Task Force to launch an evening raid, to help reduce pressure on the US Fifth Fleet off Okinawa. Rawlings agreed, despite the weather conditions. However, at 1530hrs, when the strike was due to be launched, it was cancelled owing to the near-impossible flying conditions. Rawlings was forced to send his regrets to the American admiral. However, a planned American strike on Miyako, to be carried out by shore-based bombers operating from Okinawa at 1700hrs that afternoon, was also cancelled for the same reason.

By dawn on Monday 21 May, conditions over the Sakishimas had improved and the Carrier Group was able to launch five strikes, the first taking off for Miyako at 0655hrs. Each island was targeted by alternate strikes, with the 0835hrs strike hitting Ishigaki, the 1210hrs one Miyako, the 1440hrs one Ishigaki and the final one at 1610hrs attacking Miyako. Low cloud over both islands made bombing tricky, but by the end of the day's strikes, both Ishigaki Main and Hirara were out of action after some heavy bombing, Nobara was badly damaged and Miyara had been hit, although the post-strike reconnaissance flight was unable to examine the damage due to the cloud. Only one enemy aircraft was detected all day, a reconnaissance plane which was shot down 36 miles south-west of the Task Force.

Shortly before sunset, the fleet broke off and headed south again to rendezvous at Cootie. During the run south, Rawlings digested a signal from Adm. Halsey, who was due to take over from Adm. Spruance. Interestingly, the fleet remained the same, only the senior commanders changed, together with their staffs, and the fleet's name too. When Halsey took over, the Fifth Fleet would become the Third Fleet. Halsey told Fraser and Rawlings that the BPF had done well, and he wanted to continue to have it fight alongside him as he continued his drive towards the Japanese homeland. The British commanders of course, were delighted, as after a period of refit and repair, TF 57 would remain close to the heart of the action during this final naval campaign of the war.

First though, Rawlings and his men had to finish their current job – the neutralizing of the Sakishimas. At Rendezvous Area Cootie, *Formidable* was detached on 22 May, protected by two destroyers from the Fleet Train. The carrier would stop at Manus, before continuing on to Sydney, where she would undergo urgent repairs. Replacement aircraft were transferred to the remaining three fleet carriers, although two Hellcats crashed during the transfer – a reflection of the lack of experience of some of the replacement pilots. Refuelling continued into the next day, but that evening TF 57 departed from Cootie, and returned to the Sakishimas for the final time. This time though, Vian only had three carriers under his command.

Rawlings had hoped to finish with a flourish, by bombarding Miyako for the second time. However, with the reduced number of fighters available to the Task Force, Vian argued that he lacked the ability to provide a strong CAP screen over both the Bombardment Force and the Carrier Group. So, Rawlings and Vian agreed to complete the fleet's two-month long operational tour in the Central Pacific in a less spectacular fashion, with air strikes. Even then, bad weather in the shape of low cloud, overcast skies, rain and fog led to the planned four strikes over the next two days being reduced to three.

On Thursday 24 May, the weather led to the first attacks being postponed until 1045hrs. It was the first of two strikes on Miyako, the second being launched at 1515hrs. In between, a strike against Ishigaki would be sent off at 1245hrs. However, the three strikes that followed caused considerable damage, largely because the Avengers were carrying American 1,600lb

V. Adm. Sir Philip Vian (1894–1968) was a bona-fide naval hero, having earned a reputation as an aggressive yet highly intelligent naval commander in actions against the Germans and Italians. However, in the Pacific his role was very different: leading Britain's most potent carrier strike force of the war. He proved himself a natural at fast carrier operations.

AP Mark I bombs, which were much better suited to cratering runways that their British counterparts. By Thursday evening, both Hirara airfield and the adjacent town had been badly damaged. The bombers even managed to wreck two Japanese aircraft. Ishigaki Main had also been pounded hard and all of its runways were put out of action.

On Friday 25 May, the final day of the Sakishima operation for TF 57, the poor weather cleared slightly before dawn, and the first strike of the day was launched at 0600hrs, ten minutes after sunrise. All three carriers were involved in these two days of strikes, as everyone wanted to play their part in this final phase of the operation. In this case, on each day each carrier supplied a third of each strike and escort. The day's operations began with a strike against Miyako taking off at 0600hrs, followed by an Ishigaki strike at 1115hrs and a final Miyako strike at 1400hrs. Low cloud and rain over both islands proved a problem, but Nobara was rendered completely unserviceable, being churned up by 1,600lb bombs, while 14 more hits were achieved on Hirara's runways. On Ishigaki, eight of these powerful bombs cratered Ishigaki Main and another eight did the same to Miyara airfield.

This marked the end of a long and frustrating operation. Despite the poor flying conditions over the past two days, no aircraft had been lost. While the US Fifth Fleet bore the main brunt of the Okinawa operation, and suffered the bulk of the kamikaze attacks, TF 57 had played a more mundane part, albeit an important one. Regularly bombing the same airfields might have seemed like a pointless exercise at times, but the denial of the Sakishima airfields to the kamikazes probably saved the US Fifth Fleet from far greater losses than it suffered. So, at 1900hrs, when V. Adm. Rawlings ordered the Task Force to break off and set a course towards Rendezvous Area Cootie, he must have felt satisfied that he and his fleet had carried out their duty well, and despite setbacks they, as Pacific novices, had matched the exacting standards set by the US Navy.

Three hours later, at 2200hrs, Rawlings handed over command of the Task Force to R. Adm. Vian. Then Rawlings' flagship *King George V* detached itself and steamed away to the south-west, escorted by three destroyers. Rawlings was heading to Guam, to the north-east of Ulithi, where he would meet Nimitz and Spruance for an operational debriefing. Then he would discuss the BPF's participation in the final phase of the Pacific War. Meanwhile, Vian led the battle-weary ships of TF 57 south. After refuelling at Cootie, the BPF would head to its forward base at Manus, before dispersing to various Australian ports for repairs, refits and replenishment. As Vian's Task Force completed its replenishment at Cootie, a signal arrived from Adm. Spruance, which had been passed on by Rawlings.

It read: 'On completion of your two months' operations as a Task Force of the Fifth Fleet in support of the capture of Okinawa, I wish to express to you and to the officers and men under your command, my appreciation of the fine work you have done and the splendid spirit of cooperation with which you have done it.' Spruance though, had saved the best compliment for last: 'To the American portion of the Fifth Fleet, Task Force 57 has typified the great traditions of the Royal Navy.' Coming from a veteran fighting admiral of the US Navy, there was arguably no finer compliment than that.

AFTERMATH AND ANALYSIS

This ringing endorsement from Adm. Spruance pleased the men of TF 57, and it played well at home. However, there was no avoiding the fact that the British part in Operation *Iceberg* was a relatively minor one. The Sakishima Islands, at the south-west end of the Ryukyu island chain, were at least 150 miles from Okinawa, and the attacks there, while important to the success of the Okinawa operation, were still something of a sideshow. While the bulk of the US Fifth Fleet had spent several weeks locked in battle with waves of kamikazes, TF 57 had had a less frenetic time of it – for much of the air campaign it had faced no real opposition. This though, didn't take into account two ferocious kamikaze attacks launched against it in the latter stages of the campaign, and the fact that, despite everything, the British Task Force remained in action for the best part of two months, operating thousands of miles from its base.

For the first time since 1940, a British fleet had been able to impose control of the water and skies in which it operated and impose its will on the enemy. This marked an end of that long and costly trail that stretched from Norway, Dunkirk and Greece to the fall of Crete and the Malta Convoys, and on to the Indian Ocean Raids of 1942. By May 1945, the British had a fleet which was powerful enough to dominate and win an air campaign off an enemy coast. This it did off the Sakishimas and Formosa, and so played its part in the American victory on Okinawa. While the bulk of the kamikaze strikes directed against the US Fifth Fleet came from the north – from the direction of the Japanese homeland – the most skilled Japanese pilots, and therefore the most serious kamikaze threat, lay in the west. The threat from Formosa by way of the Sakishimas was much more potent.

By dominating the skies over the Sakishimas, the Fleet Air Arm denied the Japanese an easy route from Formosa to Okinawa, by way of the Sakishima Islands. By putting the airfields on Ishigaki and Miyako out of action, and repeatedly cratering and re-cratering their runways, the British air strikes denied the use of these vital airfields to the Japanese kamikaze units. This, combined with the air attacks on northern Formosa, helped to reduce drastically the western threat to Spruance's fleet off Okinawa. While handfuls of Japanese aircraft made it

An Avenger of 849 NAS, after crashing into the island of HMS *Victorious* on landing, mid-April 1945. Amid the deck handlers inspecting the damage, a pair wielding brooms clear away the last of the debris. The aircraft was back in service two days later.

Early on 7 April, the battleship *Yamato* and nine smaller warships sailed from Kitakyushu in Japan on a kamikaze mission to take on the US Fifth Fleet. However, later that day the battleship was attacked by aircraft from US Task Group 58 and was sunk with the loss of about 3,000 of her crew. While the men of TF 57 celebrated this victory, known as the Battle of the East China Sea, they regretted not being involved in such a spectacular operation.

past the British, the powerful CAP screens established over the islands made it extremely difficult for the Japanese to carry out large-scale kamikaze attacks launched from Formosa. As a result, the British undoubtedly helped save the lives of American servicemen during the Okinawa campaign.

It had been a hard task, made even harder by the relatively poor logistical support afforded TF 57. The bombs used to crater the Sakishima runways were not really suitable, which made it necessary to fly far more bombing missions to achieve the same ends – the neutralization of the airfields – than would have been necessary if suitable ordnance had been available. Similarly, when 60lb rockets proved highly effective during the attacks on Ishigaki and Miyako, they were in short supply, and despite the urgent request made by R. Adm. Vian, suitable numbers of them never arrived from Britain in time to be used in the Okinawa campaign. The British made mistakes too. Neither Vian nor Rawlings was fully aware that by early 1945 Japanese 'Dinah' reconnaissance planes were sometimes equipped with radar, and these helped pinpoint the British Task Force. As a result, the *tokko* special attack formations knew the location and composition of the British fleet and could plan their kamikaze strikes accordingly.

It was fortunate that the kamikaze threat from the west was over-estimated by Allied intelligence. This though, was partly the result of the denial by TF 57 of the Sakishima airfields as a launch point for these attacks. Those air attacks on the US Fifth Fleet which did take place from that direction were generally thwarted by the strong American CAP screen.

A Japanese Zeke fighter is cheered as it takes off from an airfield in Kyushu, bound for the US Fifth Fleet off Okinawa. Beneath the fuselage, this kamikaze fighter carries a 250kg bomb. While this reduced the fighter's manoeuvrability in the air, it greatly increased the effectiveness of the damage inflicted by a kamikaze strike.

Interestingly, in July, 30 kamikaze attacks were launched on US warships from the Sakishima airfields, after they had been repaired. So, this threat was very real.

Before Operation *Iceberg*, Adm. Fraser had been determined that the BPF would play its full part in the Pacific War. It certainly did so during the Okinawa campaign. The Task Force had remained at sea for longer than any other British naval force in either world war. Its carriers had launched 4,893 sorties, of which 2,073 had been air strikes against Japanese targets in the Sakishimas and northern Formosa. Another 470 sorties had been flown during replenishment operations, as aircraft from the escort carriers performed CAP and ASW missions. In all, the Fleet Air Arm had dropped 959 tons of bombs, and fired 950 rockets. Essentially, it was the longest and most determined air operation in the Fleet Air Arm's history.

This though, was achieved at a cost. TF 57's carrier strike force lost 160 aircraft during the campaign, while another 43 aircraft were badly damaged, but were eventually repaired and returned to service. Of these, 26 aircraft were shot down or otherwise lost in combat, while 72 were the result of operating accidents such as crash landings or mechanical malfunction. Unsurprisingly, 66 of these involved the fragile Seafire, most of which had been lost or damaged in deck-landing accidents. Of the remainder, 32 aircraft were destroyed on their carrier's flight decks in kamikaze strikes, while another 30 aircraft were lost in the hangar fire in *Formidable*. The Fleet Air Arm lost 41 air crew killed or missing, while another 44 Task Force crewmen were killed and 83 wounded during Operation *Iceberg*. This though, is dwarfed by the US Navy's casualty list of almost 5,000 killed and almost as many wounded.

Unlike the rest of the US Fifth Fleet, TF 57 didn't lose any ships during the air campaign, but three British aircraft carriers were damaged, while a fourth suffered minor damage, which didn't require any major repairs. Interestingly, all of the British carriers had been able to remain in action after a brief period to clear their flight decks of wreckage or make good

An incredibly rare image, taken by an extremely courageous American cameraman, of the final moments of a kamikaze attack on the escort carrier USS *Sangamon*. The plane crashed into the centre of the flight deck, plunging through it to explode inside the hangar, causing extensive damage. This attack, which killed 46 men, took place on 4 May, the same day as the second round of successful kamikaze attacks on TF 57.

other repairs. This contrasts with the US Navy experience, where carriers which suffered kamikaze hits had to be withdrawn from operations, to undergo extensive repairs. This, more than anything else, was a testimony to the armoured flight deck.

Above all, during Operation *Iceberg* the British Pacific Fleet – the largest naval force assembled by the Royal Navy during World War II – had successfully taken the fight to the enemy, and by dominating the air and sea over the Sakishima Islands, had succeeded in its mission. Adm. Spruance had asked that the British neutralize the Sakishima airfields. TF 57 did that and more. It also effectively neutralized the threat to Spruance's fleet from the west, and had launched bombing attacks on Formosa, the only available launching point for kamikaze attacks following the cratering of the Sakishima airfields. In the process, TF 57 had earned praise for its actions from both Nimitz and Spruance. Even more importantly, it had proved it was capable of matching the war-hardened professionalism of the US Pacific Fleet and had shown it was worthy of fighting alongside it during the final drive to Japan. Off Okinawa that spring, the British Carrier Strike Force finally came of age.

FURTHER READING

Beaver, Paul, *The British Aircraft Carrier*, Patrick Stephens, Wellingborough (1992)

Bruhn, David, *Turn into the Wind, Vol. 1 – US Navy and Royal Navy Light Fleet Aircraft Carriers in World War II*, Heritage Books, Westminster, MD (2021)

Brown, J.D. (ed.), *The British Pacific and East Indies Fleets: The Forgotten Fleets*, Brodie Publishing, Liverpool (1995)

Brown, J.D., *Carrier Operations in World War II*, Seaforth Publishing, Barnsley (2009)

Campbell, John, *Naval Weapons of World War Two*, Conway Maritime Press, London (1985)

Chesneau, Roger, *Aircraft Carriers of the World, 1914 to the Present: An Illustrated Encyclopaedia*, Arms & Armour Press, London (1992)

Francillon, R.J., *Japanese Aircraft of the Pacific War*, Putnam, London (1979)

Friedman, Norman, *Naval Radar*, Conway Maritime Press, London (1981)

Friedman, Norman, *British Carrier Aviation: The Evolution of their Ships and their Aircraft*, Conway Maritime Press, London (1988)

Friedman, Norman, *Naval Anti-Aircraft Guns and Gunnery*, Naval Institute Press, Annapolis, MD (2014)

Foster, Simon, *Okinawa 1945: Final Assault on the Empire*, Weidenfeld, London (1994)

Gray, Edwyn, *Operation Pacific*, Pen & Sword, Barnsley (2010)

Grehan, John, *Okinawa: The Last Naval Battle of WW2: the Official Admiralty Account of Operation Iceberg*, Frontline Books, Barnsley (2022)

Hanson, Norman, *Carrier Pilot*, Silvertail Books, Kidderminster (2016)

Hobbs, David, *British Aircraft Carriers: Design, Development and Service Histories*, Seaforth Publishing, Barnsley (2013)

Hobbs, David, *Aircraft Carrier Victorious: Detailed in the Original Builders' Plans*, Seaforth Publishing, Barnsley (2018)

Hobbs, David, *The British Pacific Fleet: The Royal Navy's Most Powerful Strike Force*, Seaforth Publishing, Barnsley (2017)

Humble, Richard, *Fraser of North Cape: The Life of Admiral of the Fleet Lord Fraser*, Routledge & Kegan Paul, London (1995)

Lavery, Brian, *Churchill's Navy: The Ships, Men and Organisation, 1939–45*, Conway Maritime Press, London (2006)

Masanori, Ito, *The End of the Imperial Japanese Navy*, Weidenfeld & Nicolson, London (1962)

Ministry of Defence (Navy), *War with Japan – Vol. VI: The Advance to Japan*, HMSO, London (1995)

Morison, Samuel E., *Victory in the Pacific 1945*, History of United States Naval Operations in World War II Series, Vol. 14, Little, Brown & Co., Boston, MA (1960)

Robbins, Guy, *The Aircraft Carrier Story, 1908–1945*, Cassell & Co., London (2001)

Roskill, Stephen, *The War at Sea: The Offensive, June 1944–August 1945*, Vol. III, Part 2, HMSO, London (1961)

Smith, Peter C., *Task Force 57: The British Pacific Fleet, 1944–45*, Crecy Publishing, Manchester (2001)

Strurtivant, Ray, *British Naval Aviation*, Arms & Armour Press, London (1990)

Thetford, Owen, *British Naval Aircraft since 1912*, Putnam, London (1962)

Van der Vat, Dan, *The Pacific Campaign*, Simon & Schuster, London (1991)

Vian, Sir Philip, *Action this Day: A War Memoir*, Frederick Muller, London (1960)

Watton, Ross, *The Aircraft Carrier Victorious*, Anatomy of the Ship Series, Conway Maritime Press, London (2004)

Willmott, H.P., *Grave of a Dozen Schemes: British Naval Planning and the War Against Japan 1943–45*, Naval Institute Press, Annapolis, MD (1996)

Winton, John, *The Forgotten Fleet: Story of the British Pacific Fleet, 1944–45*, Michael Joseph, London (1969)

Winton, John, *Air Power at Sea, 1939–45*, Sedgwick & Jackson, London (1976)

INDEX

Page numbers in **bold** refer to illustrations and those in *italic* refer to tables.

air crews 5, 28, **30**, 56, 70, **70**, 71, 74, 78, 80, 91
air defence **10** (9)
air strikes and bombing raids 4, **5**, 14, **29** (28), 30, **31**, 37–38, 40, 42–43, 50, 52, **53**, 57–58, 63–64, 65, **66–67** (65), 68, 69, 75, 78–80, **79**, **80**, 84, 85–88, **85**, **86**, 89–90
  Ramrod missions 38, 40, 42–43, **44–45**, 46, 50, 51, 52, 58, 59, **59**, 62, 74
air warning defences 17, 40, 63, 68, 74
aircraft
  A6M Zero 18
  crashes 41, 50, 87, **89**, 91
  D4Y1 'Suisei' 18, 20
  Fairey Barracudas **21**
  Fairey Firefly **10**, 12, **60–61** (59), 62
  G4M1 ('Betty') 18
  Grumman Avenger **6**, 10, **27**, **28**, **33**, 36, 37–38, 40–41, 43, 58, 59, 62, **80**, 85, **89**
  Grumman Hellcat 10, 36, 37–38, 40, 42, 43, 46, **46**, 51, 54, 58, 59, **62**, 63, 68
  Japanese, numbers of 17–18, *18*, 20
  Ki-43 Hayabusa 18
  Ki-51 Sonia **60–61** (59), 62–63
  Ki-61 'Tony' 46, 59, 63
  Mitsubishi A6M Zeke 46–47, **48–49** (47), **56**, 75–77, 80–82, **91**
  Nakajima Ki-44 **15**
  Seafire 10, 12, 37, **37**, **38**, 39, **41**, 43, **48–49** (47), 50, **50**, 58, 59, 68, 80, **81**, 91
  Vought Corsair **8**, 10, **26**, **28**, 37–38, **37**, 40–41, 43, 58, 59, **59**, 63, 65, 68, 78, 85
  Yokosuka P1Y 'Ginga' bombers 34
  see also kamikaze attacks

aircraft carriers 10, 12
  aircraft lifts 37
  fast carrier operations 4, 8, 14
  operational limits 28
  paint schemes **12**, **14**
  taking off **52**, 84
airfields 22, 30, **53**, 57–58, 62, 64, **64**, 69
Andrewes, Capt. 82
Argonaut, HMS 43

Bismarck Sea, USS 24
Black Prince, HMS 74, 85
British Pacific Fleet (BPF) 4–5, 22, 24, **35**
  Carrier Strike Force 4, 14, **19** (18), 30, 34, 65, **69**, 91, 92
  deployment 13
  efficiency 14
  Fleet Train 8, 9, 26, 33, 34, 36, 42, 52, 53, 55, 68, 71, 82–83, 85
  Operational Area 8–9
  see also Task Force 57
Bunker Hill, USS 20, **83**

campaign details 33–88
  aftermath and analysis 89–92
  Day 1: 26 March 37–40
  Day 2: 27 March 40–42
  final phase 82–88
  first attacks 36–37
  kamikazes, return of 79–82
  L-Day 42–47, **44–45**, 50–53
  from Leyte to Miyako 69–79, **72–73**
  objectives of the campaign 21–31
  Operation *Iceberg Oolong* 57–59, 62–65
  order of battle 31–32
  return to the Sakishimas 65, 68–69
  tactical modifications 82–83
capabilities
  attackers 8–14
  defenders 15–20
casualties and losses 20, 38, 39, 40–41, 50, 63, 85, 91–92
chronology 6–7
Chute, Lt 37

collisions 85
Combat Air Patrol (CAP) **11**, 12, 13, 14, 36, 37, 39, 40, 43, 46–47, 55, 57, 58, 59, 63, 68, 74, 78, 90
  TarCAP **66–67** (65), 69
crews and airmen 69–71, **70**

Denny, Capt. 39, 51, 69–70, 80, 81
dogfights 62, 63

East China Sea, Battle of 90
Eccles, Capt. 36, 82
Essex, USS **13**
Euryalus, HMS 36, 71, **71**, 74

Fleet Air Arm 89, 91
  air crews **30**
  attack methods **29** (28)
  flight decks 12, **13**, 50, 84
Formidable, HMS 12, **18**, 20, **22**, 28, **55**, 65, **69**, 76–77, **76**, 78, 79, 81–82, 85, 87, 91
Formosa 17, 57–58, **60–61** (59), 89
Fraser, Adm. Sir Bruce 8, 9, 24, **34**, 69, 86–87, 91

Gambia, HMNZS 74, 75
Giran 64, **64**

Halsey Powell, USS 30
Halsey, V. Adm 24, 86–87
Hancock, USS 20, 30, 57
Hay, Lt Col. 42, 51, 62, 64
Hinsdale, USS 46
Hirara airfield **16**, **66–67** (65), 69, 79, 79–80, 84, 85–86, **85**, **86**, 88
Hitler, Adolf 79
Howe, HMS 34, 36, 74, 81

Ikishima Jima **44–45**
Illustrious, HMS **4**, **9**, 12, **26**, **33**, 37, **37**, **46**, 52, 56, 63, 65, 70, 71
Indefatigable, HMS **6**, 12, 13, **14**, 20, 28, 37, **37**, **38**, 40, **41**, **48–49** (47), 50, 56, 68, 70, 71, 77
Indomitable, HMS 12, **22**, 36, 37, 40, 46, 47, 50, 63, 68, **69**, 70, **76**, 77, **77**, 78, **78**, 81–82, 84, 85

INDEX

Intrepid, USS 20
Iwo Jima 21, 22, 28, 30

Jameson, Sub. Lt Ralph **58**
Japanese forces
    8th Air Division 17, 20
    10th Air Division 17
    Air Combat Groups 17
    Imperial Japanese Air Force 20
    Japanese Army Air Force 18
    tokko ('special attack') units 20, 90

kamikaze attacks 5, 12, 13, **19** (18), 24, 27, 34, 46, 47, **48–49** (47), 50, 51, 53–57, **54**, **55**, **56**, **57**, **60–61** (59), 63, **78**, 79–82, 88, 89–91
    damage to ships **18**, 76–77, **76**, **77**, 80–81, **83**, **92**
    threat of 20
Kempenfelt, HMS 36, 71
King, Adm. Ernest J. **22**, 24, 30
King George V, HMS 34, 37, 47, **47**, 74, 88

Leyte 69–70
logistics 8–9, 34

MacArthur, Gen. Douglas 21, 22, 57, 58
Mariana Islands 21
Maryland, USS 20, 57
Matsuyama 57–58, 62, 64
Mitscher, V. Adm 24, 27–28, 30
Morris, V. Adm. 34

Naval Air Squadrons (NAS)
    820 NAS **37**, 38, 62
    849 NAS 38, **38**, 62, 64, **66–67** (65), **80**, **89**
    854 NAS **33**, 38, 39, 41, 43, 62
    857 NAS 38, 62, **66–67** (65), **80**
    1836 NAS 38, 39
    1839 NAS 39, 63, 71
    1840 NAS 36, 70–71
    1844 NAS 39, 63
    Strike Charlie force 38–39
Nevada, USS 20
Nimitz, Adm. Chester 8, 9, **22**, 24, 26, 27, 33, 34, 36, 53, 57, 88, 92
Nobara airfield 30, 38, 42, 55, 68, 74, 75, 84, 86
Nottingham, Lt. Cdr. 41

oil production 4, **5**
Okinawa 15, 16, 17, 21–22, 26, 33, 54, 57, 89
    amphibious landing **43**, 46
Operation *Iceberg* 4, 15, 17, 20, 22, **25** (24), 26–31, 89
    British mission 27–28, 30–31
Operation *Iceberg Oolong* 57–59, 62–65
Operation *Meridian* 4
Operation *Tan 2* 34
order of battle 31–32

Palembang 4, **5**
Quickmatch, HMS **76**
Quilliam, HMS 71, **76**, 85

radar 13, 14, 16, 17, 40, 43, 75–76, 82, 90
    Airborne Early Warning Radars **10** (9)
Randolph, USS 24, 34
Rawlings, V. Adm. Bernard 26, 28, 30, 33, 34, 36, **36**, 37, 40, 41–42, 43, 46, 51, 55, 57, 63, 65, 68, 69, 74, 75, 78, 79, 82, 86–87, 88, 90
reconnaissance 42, 46, 51, 68, 78, 90
replenishment at sea (RAS) 9–10, **9**, 34, 36, 42, 53, 55–56, 79
Reynolds, Sub. Lt 'Dicky' **48–49** (47), 50
Roosevelt, Franklin D. 64
Royal Fleet Auxiliary (RFA) 10
Ryukyu Islands 18

Sakishima 15–17, 27, 42–43, 46, 51–53, 57, 65, 68–69, 74, 83, 89, 92
    Ishigaki Jima 16–17, 74, 84, 86, 88, 89
    Miyako Jima 16, **16**, 65, **66–67** (65), 68, 69, **72–73**, 78, 84, 86, 87–88, 89
    surrender of **51**
Sakishima military defences, Ishigaki Jima garrison 16–17, 55, **79**, **80**
Sangamon, USS **92**
Saratoga, USS 24
Shinchiku 57–58, 62, 64
Speaker, HMS 36, 42, 70–71, 79
Sprague, R. Adm. 42, 57

Spruance, Adm. Raymond 5, 8, 9, **22**, 24, 26, 53, 57, 63, 64, 68, **84**, 88, 92
Striker, HMS 36, 42
submarines 41, 43, 58
suicide crash boats 0
Sukuma airfield 30, 55, 68, 74, 75
Sumatra 4, **5**, 8
Swiftsure, HMS 37, 74

Task Force 50 27
Task Force 52 26, 52, 58
Task Force 54 26–27
Task Force 57 5, 14, 20, 26, 30, 36, 40, 43, 46, 51, 53, 54–57, 57, 58, 63–65, 68–69, **69**, 71, 74–75, 78–80, 82–88, 89, 90, 91–92
    cruising formation **25** (24), 37, 83
Task Force 58 24, 26, 27–28, 30, 34
Tennessee, USS 20
Tomkinson, Lt. Cdr. 38
Turner, V. Adm 26

Ugaki, V. Adm. Matome 20
Uganda, HMCS 56, 71
Ujujima, Gen. Mitsuru 15
Unicorn, HMS **69**, 71
US Fifth Air Force 58
US Navy 4–5, 8, **9**, 20, 21, 22
    Fifth Fleet 33–34, **35**, 36, 63, 86–87, 88, 89, 90, 92

Vian, V. Adm. Sir Philip 28, 31, 33, 34, 37–38, 40, 42, 56, 58, 65, 68, **70**, 78, 82, 87, **87**, 88, 90
Victorious, HMS 12, **12**, 20, 36, 37, **37**, 51, 52, 63, **69**, 70, **70**, 78, 80–81, **82**, **84**, **89**

Wager, HMS 43
weapons
    AA defences **11**, 14, 17, 38, **75**, 76, 77, **77**, 84
    bombs **33**, 38, **42**, 43, 55, 87–88, 90, **91**
    gun bombardments 75
    rockets 38, 69, 90, 91
weather problems 41–42, 79, 85, 86, 87
Whirlwind, HMS 36, 71

Yamato **90**
Yasuda, Lt Gen. Takeo 17